❖ ❖ ❖

How to
Make Money
in the
Antiques-and-Collectibles
Business

by
Elyse Sommer

ILLUSTRATED WITH PHOTOGRAPHS

Houghton Mifflin Company
Boston
1979

Library of Congress Cataloging in Publication Data
Sommer, Elyse.
How to make money in the
antiques-and-collectibles business.
Bibliography: p.
1. Antique dealers.   2. Antiques—Marketing.
3. Antiques as an investment.   I. Title.
NK1133.S65   381'.45'74510973   78-25568
ISBN 0-395-27758-2

Printed in the United States of America

V 10 9 8 7 6 5 4 3 2 1

Book design by Marty Lehtola, Designworks, Inc.

Also by Elyse Sommer
Decoupage Old and New
Rock and Stone Craft
Contemporary Costume Jewelry
The Bread Dough Craft Book
Designing with Cutouts
Make It with Burlap
Inventive Fiber Crafts
Career Opportunities in Crafts
Textile Collector's Guide

By Elyse and Mike Sommer
Creating with Driftwood and Weathered Wood
A New Look at Crochet
A New Look at Felt
Wearable Crafts
A New Look at Knitting

by Elyse Sommer with Joellen Sommer
Sew Your Own Accessories
A Patchwork, Appliqué and Quilting Primer

By Elyse Sommer and Renie Breskin Adams
Pillowmaking as Art and Craft

❖ ❖ ❖

How to
Make Money
in the
Antiques-and-Collectibles
Business

❖ ❖ ❖

Foreword
and
Acknowledgments

Subconsciously, I've been writing this book since I saved the covers from my Dixie ice-cream containers and spent most of my allowance on movie-star photographs. This subconscious process continued through the period when I feathered my first adult nest, buying antique furniture and textiles because they were cheaper than new things. In retrospect, I realize I would have chosen to shop in antique stores and auction rooms rather than new-furnishings showrooms no matter what my budget.

On a conscious level, a specific plan for this book began to take form while I was writing two others — one on the crafts profession and another on textile collecting and collectors.

In terms of actual work, I've spent almost a year talking to and corresponding with professionals in all walks of the collecting world. A mere thank you hardly suffices for their generosity in sharing knowledge, brainstorming ideas, and leading me to other sources. The names of many of these nice and knowledgeable people appear throughout the book, along with the more indirectly reflected thoughts of hundreds of anonymous "collaborators." I thank them one and all. The size of the antiques-collectibles business precluded my working with more than a sampling, if this was to be anything short of a lifetime endeavor.

In addition to the many individuals who responded patiently to my inquiries, I wish to express my thanks to the antiques-collectibles fourth estate, for giving space to my interview needs and for making their publications available for study and review. I am particularly grateful to Mrs. Gray D. Boone for affording me the opportunity to partake in *The Antique Monthly*'s annual conference at the Hotel Pierre in New York City. Special thanks are owed to Mr. Bob Gittleman, of Hunter College's Lifelong Learning Center, for inviting me to monitor one of a series of two-day business seminars, and to Mr. Dexter MacBride, of the American Society of Appraisers, for making available so much of his organization's educational materials. Thank you, Audrey Brandes, for connecting me with your particular network of antiques professionals in the Long Island area, and Margaret Scholer, for similar services rendered in Minnesota.

To my husband, Mike Sommer, I'd like to offer formal acknowledgment of what he already knows — that without his camera, company during long drives, and feedback on ideas and interviews, this book would probably still be in the think tank. A final thanks to my editor, Frances Tenenbaum, for having the vision to support this project when it was not much more than "a good idea" and for seeing the final manuscript through the many stages from the day of submission to the day of publication.

❖ ❖ ❖

Contents

PART II   Resources

9   In-Print Information   **161**

10   Advertising and Promotion Guidelines   **179**

11   Photography Know-How   **182**

12   Legal Matters   **184**

13   People and Places for Guidance and Education   **189**

Glossary of Antiques Trade Jargon   **194**

Index   **207**

❖ ❖ ❖

Introduction

It is not the purpose of this book to analyze the intrinsic value of the many different types of objects that are collected today. The title includes antiques and collectibles because both are key components of an annual buying and selling total of twelve *billion* dollars! Without collectibles, the so-called collecting boom would be no more than a modest boomlet.

For many, especially the old-time antiques dealers, the interrelationship between antiques and collectibles represents more of a shotgun marriage than a love affair. Yet without the lobbying efforts of a good many of these same early dealers, the customs office might still legally accept as antiques only objects produced before 1830. The more flexible definition of an antique as anything 100 years old, signed into law in Great Britain in 1959 and in the United States in 1966, although designed primarily to relieve import duties, did much to democratize antiques. Collecting became much more varied and enlarged its embrace. The backlash in the late sixties against an increasingly stereotyped environment further enlarged the nature of, as well as people's attitude toward, collecting. Since discontent with the environment often extended to the work experience, it was only natural that many saw in collecting not just an avocational form of self-expression but a real opportunity for a vocation. And so a whole new class of professionals came into being, and it was their energies that led to the boom.

The new professionals did not actually invent antiques-related careers. Dealers, auctioneers, property appraisers, restorers, and conservators have been around for years. So have writers of books and articles on art and antiques, and promoters of lectures and shows. What *is* new is the number and the nature of the people who are "in the business." Show impresarios have cropped up throughout the land, producing anywhere from two to fifty shows a year, ranging from flea markets to nostalgia shows to those featuring museum-quality displays. Permanent marketplaces, in the form of antique centers, have sprung up everywhere; these are at once a variation of the show theme and an attempt to bring the old-style antique shop into the modern marketing mainstream. Auctions are almost as ubiquitous as shops and shows, and the giants among these have brought people with public relations and advertising know-how beneath the umbrella of the antiques and collectibles business. All the aforementioned — dealers, promoters, auctioneers, and of course, buyers — have, in turn, created a market for a staggering number of publications, to keep everyone abreast of what is happening. There are currently well over fifty collector-oriented publications, not counting collectors' clubs newletters and specialized magazines. The largest proportion of these postdate 1969. Add to this a never-ending flow of books and newspaper columns, and it becomes clear that publishing not only informs, but provides its own primary and secondary career opportunities within the antiques-collectibles field.

With so many enthusiasms at work, it is indeed a wonder that, although library shelves overflow with books on how to collect everything imaginable, little or nothing has been written specifically for and about those who make up the industry that keeps the collecting wheels in motion. By focusing on the people behind the objects, the professionals, *The Antiques-and-Collectibles Business* should enable would-be professionals to gain the knowledge necessary to cross the bridge from avocation to vocation, and to help those already in the business to expand their horizons. As already stated, this is an overview of the professional structure, not a judgmental analysis of the esthetics of one or another phase of the business. The book is a segment in what I perceive as an emerging trend; namely, more and better education for selling, service, and managerial careers. The questions addressed are the ones most frequently raised: What do the different types of full-time and part-time job and business situations entail? What are the money, management, and marketing problems to be anticipated and resolved? What support organizations, education programs, and ongoing sources of published information are available?

I hope the answers here will help fledgling professionals decide whether and how they should get started, and show those who have already tested the waters how to keep going. It may help them, too, in considering alternative or additional income opportunities.

Probably more people want to be, and are, dealers than anything else, but there are many types of dealerships. Several endeavors can be combined, to provide increased and steadier incomes or to expand one's activities into a multifaceted career. It is hoped that this book will encourage you to try on the many hats worn by those people already "in" antiques and collectibles. Whether the shop dealer's or the show dealer's hat seems to suit you better, or whether your hand itches to hold the auctioneer's gavel, familiarize yourself with the problems and functions of each professional. The methods of one can be adapted to the needs of the other. The paths of almost all will cross at one point or another, and a greater mutual understanding and sharing can only help to foster individual as well as overall effectiveness.

As Stella Hall, editor of *The Antiques Dealer*, cautioned in an editorial in her March 1978 issue: "Remember — appraiser, auctioneer, restorer, retailer, shipper, show manager, wholesaler, even trade magazine editor — whatever limb of the antiques tree you may be out on, we're all in this together."

It is unquestionably true that this business, more than any other, defies a step-by-step success approach. Thus, though there are tips and role models throughout these pages, it is no more possible to offer economy-proof, sure-fire formulas than it is to predict beyond reasonable doubt which products from either past or present will be successful, even spectacular, investments for the future.

Some final points about the organization and use of this book:

Arrangement according to major functional or role categories was dictated by the need to present information in the most readable and accessible way. Many discussions in one chapter could easily fit into another, so a complete reading, no matter what your particular interest, is suggested. Part II, the Resource section, is a vital part of the whole and is intended as a ready and constant reference.

The ultimate value of this book rests with you, the reader. Anyone who gains some help or insight, does something new or different, will be writing his or her own postscript. If you would like to share your experiences — or comments, questions, criticisms — the learning and enjoyment that accompanied the writing of this book will become a continuing pleasure.

Elyse Sommer
P.O. Box E
Woodmere, New York 11598

PART I

❖ ❖ ❖

The Structure of the Business: Who Does What, When, and Where

CHAPTER 1

❖ ❖ ❖

Yesterday a Buyer,
Today a Dealer

The classic beginning in any antiques business is at the moment when you make your first purchase. Then more and more and more until out of sheer necessity — and to make money so you can buy more antiques — you find yourself in business, with high hopes and a resale number.
— Alton Ketchum, Collector-turned-dealer of old manuscripts

The oft-heard definition of a dealer as a "collector-turned-pro" is validated by the intrinsic nature of collecting, which inevitably involves dealing. You sell off your early mistakes and trade up. You buy extras to sell in order to "support your habit." Furthermore, in antiques, as in no other business, the hobbyist and the dealer buy from the same sources, read the same publications, attend the same conferences and seminars.

Anyone buying modern furniture and bathroom fixtures reads up on possible choices in a variety of consumer magazines, such as *Good Housekeeping* or *House Beautiful,* or in the decorating sections of a newspaper. He is unlikely to read *The Plumbing and Heating Wholesaler* or *The Interior Decorator's Handbook.* If he visits shows, they will be consumer-geared home-decorating shows. Trade shows are strictly wholesale.

In the antiques-collectibles world, everybody drinks from the same fountain of knowledge and mines the same sources. (Trade show activity does exist before general show openings, and, in fact, many people become exhibitors strictly to partake of this preshow action.) No wonder that so many buyers feel they are part of the trade and soon find themselves fantasizing about chucking regular jobs in pursuit of an antiques career. Many do go from fantasy to reality. Add to the dropouts from "ordinary" jobs and educational programs the growing regiments of able-bodied retirees, housewives eager to do something besides keep house, and an impressive number of second-generation dealers — and the mystery as to why there seem almost as many Antiques as McDonald's signs dotting city and country landscapes begins to clear.

For many, the dream of being a dealer turns somewhat sour in the day-to-day reality of attracting customers, turning stock over often enough and at a fair enough markup to stay on the black side of the ledger, and obtaining replacement inventory that won't eat into the earnings of the previous lot. The very growth that attracted dealers to the business in the beginning also carried the seeds of problems with competition for both customers and merchandise. Societal problems, such as thefts, holdups, fuel shortages, inflation, and economic downturns, do not by-pass the antiques-collectibles trade. (But, then, to look at the rosy side, the bad tidings of inflation are great for the antiques business!) Most important, though the transition from collector to dealer may seem as natural as breathing, surviving in this as in any business requires sound management practices. Buying at auction, for example, may be fine for the collector, but the dealer must weigh the profits from his buys at the auction against the time he invests in being there. By the same token, buying overseas must be measured in terms of shipping and time costs and additional markup, unless the trip is combined with a vacation.

Dealing in old objects does not preclude new marketing methods. The antiques dealer's inventory may resist "typical" retailing analysis, but this by no means makes inventory study or a business plan unnecessary.

Even those who become dealers without any real need to consider the bottom line — for example, retirees looking for supplemental rather than full self-support income — should plan their goals and the best ways to achieve them. All too many who want to make a leap into self-support-and-better status remain stuck in that twilight zone between avocation and vocation, simply because they haven't figured out how to move from one to the other.

BEFORE YOU GO INTO BUSINESS

What exactly is a business plan?

Quite simply, it is an assessment of your qualifications, assets, lifestyle, and goals made *before* you go into business. A plan can be a formal and lengthy analysis of all aspects of the business, such as organization, overall concept, merchandise acquisition and sales plans, accounting and legal aspects, labor costs, promotion, advertising, and a study of the competition. If you send $1.00 to the Urban Affairs Section of the Federal Reserve Bank, Boston, Massachusetts 02106, it will send you an excellent book entitled *Business Planning Guide*. With this in hand, you will be able to write up the kind of plan most likely to impress your local banker if and when the time comes for you to apply for a loan.

The business plan can also be a briefer and more informal documentation of your strengths and weaknesses, a checklist to guide your first steps, and a memorandum to be reconsidered and revised periodically. To formulate a plan like this, designed primarily for your own eyes and use, get yourself a looseleaf notebook and divide it up as follows:

Self Assessment
Research
Money
Organization and Outlook

SELF-ASSESSMENT

It's not only the most difficult thing to know oneself, but the most inconvenient.

— Josh Billings

Not everyone is suited to being an entrepreneur. The monetary rewards are often slow in coming and, when they do, are more likely to be modest than fantastic. The demands, on the other hand, are heavy. The antiques dealer constantly must make decisions about buying and buying *right,* must back up taste with knowledge, and be willing to generate the kind of enthusiasm that dims the dividing line between business and pleasure, so that the long hours seem worthwhile. The following questions are designed to help you estimate your success quotient. The first ten call for Yes or No answers; the last two, for fill-ins. Don't play the reaching-for-the-right-answer game; be totally honest. This is *your* business, *your* life!

Self-Assessment Quiz

1. Do you have any job or business experience that can be applied to your own dealership?
2. Do you look on selling as considerably less creative and enjoyable than buying?
3. Do you enjoy other people and feel responsive to their needs?
4. Do you like to read?
5. Can you make on-the-spot decisions?
6. Does record-keeping turn you off?
7. Are you the sort of person who takes the initiative, or do you wait for events to take their course?
8. Do you manage your time well?
9. Do you tend to gloss over your weaknesses?
10. Do you have lots of physical energy?
11. Can you list at least three general skills, not specifically related to antiques or collectibles, that you feel would enhance your effectiveness as a dealer?
12. Do you have any art or crafts skills that would help your business? If not, can you name at least one you think you could learn?

Analyzing Your Responses

Practical experience comes from actual doing. Mistakes by a collector hurt him where he does not forget it, right in his pocketbook. If experience is a prerequisite to proper knowledge and it is hard to get a job with a dealer, working for an auctioneer or being a collector oneself are alternatives.
> — Samuel L. Lowe, Jr., Antiques, Inc.,
> Boston, Massachusetts

I worked in a bank, which I hated. I worked for an auction gallery as a runner, which I liked. Now I'm on my own, and I can't imagine ever working for someone else again . . . though without my past jobs I would have neither the needed knowledge nor appreciation for my business.
> — Peter Rakelbusch, 21st Century Antiques,
> Hadley, Massachusetts

1. A previous job in an antiques business — the busier, the better — is an incalculable plus. This is not always easy to obtain, since most antiques businesses are run by a small number of people. If you are short of actual experience but have run a business of your own or have experience in sales or buying, you will not come as a stranger to management duties and the ability to size up people; you will know how to be friendly without becoming overly involved; and you will understand how and when to close a deal. If your answer to this question is a flat No, a business counselor would urge you to wait until you've gained at least some experience.

Good buying is know what you can sell.
> — Bruce Cummings, Antiques: A Joint Venture,
> Hadley, Massachusetts

2. A collector can afford to enjoy buying for his own pleasure, but if your answer to this question is Yes, you've got only half of what it takes to be a successful dealer-buyer.

To take Bruce Cummings' simple definition a step farther, what you buy and how well also depends on knowing *where* you can sell it. Buying well often means buying something in a geographic area where it is not highly valued and taking it to a marketplace where it is.

Browsers should not be made to feel that they are being ignored,
nor should they be made to feel that they are intruding on a
dealer who is bogged down in Joyce Carol Oates' latest novel.
— Joe Stamps, Funchies, Bunkers, Gaks and
Gleeks, at the Manhattan Art and Antiques
Center, New York City

3. The answer here should be Yes, for both buying and selling
involve dealing tactfully and astutely with people. The dealer who
tolerates people just long enough to conclude a sale is the one least
likely to sell. Part of selling is understanding customer psychology,
and this is best learned through listening and conversation.

I read and study at least two hours a day the many publications
I take [nineteen], and I spend at least five hundred dollars per
year upgrading my extensive antique book library.
— Mary Colby, Colby Antiques,
San Clemente, California

4. There wasn't one dealer interviewed during the course of my
research for this book who did not consider building a library of
periodicals and books and *using* it vital to keeping up with trends
and buying well. Ralph and Terry Kovel, outstanding examples of
the possibilities of success and fame in this business, cite their 5000–
volume library as corroboration of authenticity and therefore a major
selling point for their monthly tip sheet, *Kovels on Antiques and Collectibles*. Being well-read doesn't end with the myriad offerings on
antiques. If the *Wall Street Journal, Business Week, Kiplinger's,* home-
decorating and fashion trade and consumer publications think your
business is important enough to watch and write about (as they do,
with increasing regularity), it follows that you can in turn pick up
valuable economic and taste trends from them.

Mrs. Colby, whose "retirement" business includes two shops and
a large warehouse with six employees, commented: "There is a great
need for young people to start in fine shops and work more or less as
apprentices under knowledgeable people, learning a profession. We
start 'learners' at minimum wage, work them up to four-fifty an
hour-plus, as they learn to sell. When I take someone new in my
organization, I look for intelligence, a willingness to learn and read

my vast library, and a natural ability to sell. Perhaps the ability to sell should be put first, because unless one is running a museum, a well-informed person who can't sell is actually a detriment."

> Through several tearful experiences, I've learned not to say "I'll think about it and let you know" . . . that is, unless you find it pleasant to cry!
> — Patricia Hyde McDaniel, Tumbleweed
> Antiques, Connersville, Indiana

5. Yes, you should be able to make on-the-spot decisions, especially for buying. These decisions entail less risk for those who have lots of knowledge about market trends and quality.

This sampling of books and periodicals demanding the attention of the well-read antiques professional represents the mere tip of the iceberg.

Keeping records is the difference between GUESSTIMATING and estimating and planning.
— Bernard Kamaroff, C.P.A., in
Small-Time Operator, Bell Springs Publishing,
Laytonville, California

6. Although you don't have to be as turned on to record-keeping as to objects you buy and sell, your answer to this question should nevertheless be No. The whole secret is to keep up with your moves and to recognize bookkeeping as an aid instead of a bother, your only true key to evaluating properly your inventory and cash flow. To do this, you must record separately personal and business expenses, and should analyze regularly both costs and turnover. Does it really pay to hold on to all unsold inventory in anticipation of rising prices, without consideration of the risk of wear and breakage? Why not look at your business records with a long-range view and estimate your cash-flow picture on the basis of devaluating at least a percentage of inventory each year? Unless you make a practice of keeping accurate and regularly evaluated records, the dollar implications behind this kind of thinking will be lost on you. Instead, the danger signals of failure are likely to sneak up on you, and you'll have a going-out-of-business sale before you can consider an end-of-the-year markdown and good-will promotion.

For the antiques dealer, record-keeping goes far beyond ordinary bookkeeping. It includes maintaining clear, accessible files of buying sources, customer wants, addresses, articles, and so on. If a dealer handles consignments, records of such transactions and written agreements are good business. (See Part II, Resources.)

7. Initiative runs a close second to knowledge for success in antiques. It takes initiative to attract customers. Instead of sitting back and waiting, you have to join and become active in organizations, give talks, or arrange for displays of choice merchandise in a local restaurant or a museum.

It takes initiative to make good connections for buying, especially if you don't have them automatically. Want ads in local papers and notices tacked to store bulletin boards have brought results for many. Using initiative as a buyer can be as simple as asking to see more instead of assuming that what is visible in another dealer's shop or in a home is all there is.

8. The question of time management should be answered with a noncheating Yes. Although this may seem to belong in a corporate management handbook, most people I've met, including antiques dealers, are anxious about their time. How can they get to more shows, read more, spend more time going over customer lists, take part in lectures? How is it that some manage to do all these things and more?

Making and using lists is a great time management standby. If you want to cover every tag sale and garage sale within a fifty-mile radius or more in one weekend, write them all down. Reorder your list to eliminate unnecessary zigzagging. Use the telephone the day before to sift out the least likely possibilities. When it comes to choosing shows, spend more rather than less time in research to find out which will be best for you and which are likely to be psychically and economically draining.

Learn to get the most mileage out of everything you do. If you take an out-of-town buying trip, take lots of cards along, with your specific buying interests written on the back, and leave these as reminders wherever you go. Once the contact has been made, follow the trip up by sending other cards periodically. Timing your activities properly also helps to give more stretch to your time. For example, if you buy from other dealers, arrange to call on them during their slow season (not every snowbound country dealer is on the beach in Florida or Hawaii), when there is less interruption from retail business.

> The most cost-effective way for a businessman to improve is to pay attention to his *weakest* points, not his strongest points. This ability to concentrate on weaknesses is an advantage of small business over large business.
> — The Country Business Brokers,
>   Brattleboro, Vermont

9. The answer to this should be No. Business counselors generally seek to help you identify your strengths and build upon them, and rightly so. However, even the strongest swimmer can drown if he drifts into quicksand. If you are too weak in too many areas, don't gloss over your weaknesses, or they will swallow up your strengths.

10. Yes, you do need lots of physical energy. The modern, money-making antiques dealer spends very little time sitting in a shop doing crossword puzzles. Being in the trade requires enormous physical as well as mental stamina — driving to buy, to partake in shows, packing and unpacking merchandise, going out at odd hours when the opportunity knocks for an interesting estate. One way of strengthening a weak physical constitution is to get together with a more energetic partner.

11. If you aren't able to include three or more of the following skills in your repertoire of general assets, all is not lost. Just as there are many helpful publications that can help you and evaluate merchandise, there are many self-help manuals, as well as short and inexpensive courses in these skills: typing, basic bookkeeping, photography, speed reading, library research, copywriting, publicity writing and methods, article or filler writing, public speaking, window and interior display, auto repair and maintenance, and languages (especially German and Italian).

12. Many dealers would have to go out of business if they tried to deal only in "mint," or perfect condition, merchandise. Good restorers are much sought after, and the dealer with at least one restoration skill usually enjoys increased business and profit, and also avoids the boredom and financial frustration that accompany slow periods. Chair caning, refinishing, stenciling, china and porcelain repairing — the list of possibilities is long, as are the sources of help in the form of books and courses. (See Part II, Resources.) A bent for drawing or sketching can, of course, be used to enhance your business stationery, ads, promotional materials, and display signs. As with question 11, a positive response to this one is a definite plus.

Summing Up Your Self-Assessment Quiz

You've no doubt guessed that the more of the above questions you answered correctly, the better your chances of success. If you've got just a few negative or wrong ones, incorporate them into your plan as things to work on, to improve, to learn. If you've struck out on all twelve counts, you'd better reconsider very carefully your reasons for wanting to be a dealer.

RESEARCH

Experience is something you get too late to do anything about
the mistakes you made while getting it.

— Anon.

Under research comes any and all information you can gather on
what it takes to run a business of the type you have in mind, and
learning about trade, taste, and buying trends. Research includes
talking to individuals in the business and actually trying out the
role, either as a paid employee or as a volunteer.

A Business Bought at Auction: Research or Rashness?

Laura Fisher's entry into the retail antiques business came about
through a bid called in to the Channel 13 auction, New York's public
television fundraiser.

An extreme example of impulse or auction fever rather than careful
research before going into business?

Not really. Laura's winning bid on three months of free space at
one of New York's largest antique centers provided her with the sort
of on-site, firsthand information she felt she needed before she
turned a someday fantasy into reality. Laura's dream was to be the
proprietor of a shop where she could sell the kind of primitive,
handcrafted Americana objects she had been collecting for about five
years. The winning bid actually culminated other research activities,
for Laura had previously gained both experience and dealer friends
by selling some of her collected extras at weekend flea markets. She
had also improved her know-how by taking courses in American
folk art at the New School and at New York University.

The three months of free tenancy at the antique center marked the
beginning of a more serious commitment to being a shopkeeper.
Furthermore, coming as it did during July, August, and September,
the period did not require Laura to make any final decisions about
her job as a publicist for the New York City Human Rights Commission — a job she liked and enjoyed, even while she dreamed of
being an antiques dealer. The summer tenancy enabled Laura to
cover both her options by enlisting the help of friends who were free
for the summer and willing to "shop sit" during the week in order to

research their own interests and selling abilities. This also solved the problem of maintaining a well-stocked booth, because these other researchers added merchandise of their own on consignment.

What did the three-month period bring to light for Laura Fisher? It enabled her to understand the pattern and rhythm of retailing — a good first month, a typically slow August, and a September of recovery. It enabled Laura to weigh the pros of being in a center (safety, companionship, lower rent than an individual shop, learning from other dealers) as well as the cons (loss of street traffic, limitations of space). Moreover, though three months in business did not begin to equal three months of paychecks, Laura found that she could juggle both her careers without feeling undue strain. And so she decided to continue beyond the auctioned free tenancy, this time with one friend acting as a partner during the week in return for his being able to sell his own things.

After six months of this on-the-spot research, Laura moved into a larger space — a real shop instead of an open booth — in another center, the Manhattan Art and Antiques Center. She still did not quit her job, but she cut it down to a part-time level so that she could be in the shop four days a week and spend more time buying.

Her goal at the moment is to make the shop so successful that she'll have to quit her job altogether, though she feels even then she would always want to do some free-lance publicity work.

The chance actually to market-research your own potential business for a minimal cash outlay like Laura Fisher's auction bid isn't likely to come along every day of the week. However, the opportunity to work in a shop for pay, as a volunteer, or on a time-consignment basis can be ferreted out. If you can't find an antiques dealer to take you on, volunteer your services in a busy thrift shop. Most of the wares will probably be ordinary secondhand goods, but there's a lot to learn. One-day and weekend shows are also good places to learn and get to know other dealers, analyze your own selling abilities and forbearance under pressure. Here, too, you might help someone else set up and mind a booth, rather than wing it on your own. As for auction houses — though the large auction organizations in cities have limited openings, small country auction houses do put on part-time or volunteer runners, many of whom make good use of everything they learn. (See Chapter 5.)

Another way to get lots of information fast is to pay a consultant. You don't need a high-fee corporate consultant; he or she can be a person established in the kind of business you'd like to have — someone successful but not in a particularly competitive situation. Dealers, in spite of competition, tend to be generally helpful and encouraging to newcomers, and you will be amazed at the difference and quality of the advice you get when you treat the other person *and yourself* as professionals. If you pick your consultant wisely and

A partial view of Laura Fisher's Country Things Shop in the Manhattan Art and Antiques Center, New York City. That's Laura holding the quilt.

arm yourself with solid questions, a couple of days at, say, $100 a day, are likely to bring you more than your money's worth.

If you are planning to relocate, take advantage of the Chamber of Commerce, the local bank, and the Small Business Administration's Service Corps of Retired Executives (SCORE) to give you a financial picture of the area and to put you in touch with other business people.

MONEY

Of paramount importance, of course, is the question of how much money you will need to get going, keep afloat, and finally to grow. Just what does it take to be properly capitalized? Are all shoestring operations doomed to failure?

From my discussions with dealers, old and new, throughout the country, for every story I heard of a $500 inventory parlayed into a fortune, or even a reasonable income, I heard hundreds about businesses at or below the marginal level because of undercapitalization. The figure of $5000, as rock-bottom minimum inventory investment to start, came up often and steadily enough to make it worth repeating. However, those who deal mostly in collectibles and at shows often find $2500 adequate as a start-up. On the other hand, dealers in "true antique furnishings" tend to regard $5000 as "nothing"; they often invest at least four times that amount and build toward $50,000 to $60,000 as quickly as possible. Note, too, the term "inventory investment," since this leaves other fixed costs, such as rent and utilities, for the shop dealer; space rentals, transportation, and incidentals for the show dealer; printing and advertising for the mail order dealer — and telephone, insurance, inflationary increases, and unanticipated extras for all.

Minimum inventory is an important consideration for the dealer who meets with immediate success and is faced with the need to maintain the initial momentum. Mel Nash, of Nash Antiques in Winston-Salem, told me, "I put exactly five thousand dollars into my booth. Anything less would have been disastrous, since I would have been cleaned out before I had a chance to replenish stock."

As for projecting profits on inventory, hard-and-fast figures are particularly difficult in a business that has no established markups. The persistent spread of stories about markups of several hundred or more percent has seeded many an ill-fated business. These tales do have a foundation in fact, but they are misleading because these are not statistically averaged. The dealers with regularly high markups tend to be in that small 10 percent who deal in very expensive pieces and work with investments in the six-figure range. On the average, a given lot of merchandise may contain one or two really high-profit items, which, once sold, will pay for most of the investment. The remaining items are likely to be less than choice, disposable at markups of from 10 to 30 percent. Thus, the 30 to 50 percent markups are the most common ones for the maximum number of dealers.

If you do your research properly on projected income, your arithmetic for size of investment and markup must be carried a bit farther:

1. The markup represents *gross* earnings. Only after selling (and buying) expenses are deducted do you have a true net.

2. To project annual income, you need not only figure net earnings on a particular inventory lot, but must determine how many times this process is repeated in the course of the year. In other words, if you start with an inventory of $5000 and sell it off within six months at a 50 percent markup, you are grossing $2500 for six months. If you repeat this once again in the next six months, you have made two inventory turns, earning a gross of $5000. It now becomes clear why a large inventory and the ability to replace and turn it again is vital to even a reasonably self-supporting situation.

According to a study made by Maurice Kilbridge, published in the December 1977 issue of the *Maine Antiques Digest,* even the most successful dealers (those carrying inventories averaging $90,000) do not turn their inventories more than one and a half times in a given year. Since, according to Professor Kilbridge, these turns are made at a high markup, about 64 percent, those who are successful, or what he classifies as Big Dealers, are realizing good earnings. The Kilbridge figures on Small Dealers were far less rosy, since inventory size (approximately $20,000), turnover (.72 times a year), and markup (53 percent) were considerably smaller.

Obviously, there is a middle ground between the dealer who earns $86,000 and the one who hovers at a marginal $5000 to $7500. Editor Samuel Pennington, who published the Kilbridge survey, told me that he estimates 30 percent, or even 20 percent, to be a much more common markup for the dealers who advertise with him. However, he added that annual sales of $60,000 to $100,000 were common enough, and this would account for an existing middle range. I personally talked to a number of dealers who maintained small inventories of approximately $5000 but turned over their stock at least four to six times a year. These were mostly dealers who were out buying all the time, not confined to shops.

Both investment and earning shortcomings can be offset by those who find ways around the cash-flow problem. The most familiar is to take merchandise on consignment and earn your commissions as middleman. Here are some other ploys used by resourceful dealers:

1. Buying as an agent for a big auction house. One way to do this is to buy outright, with the auction house advancing the money plus a fee to the dealer as a finder. Another way is to bring the merchandise to the auctioneer as a consignment for a 5 percent fee of the price realized. In the latter case, the knowledgeable dealer follows up any word-of-mouth arrangement with a formal letter to auction house and consignor.

2. Dealer co-investment, which involves several dealers in one purchase. They share in the selling effort and in the final profit.

3. Option buying. This enables a dealer to gamble on something he sees in a collection that is rising in value, without a large tie-up of cash. A specified option payment holds the desired merchandise for a given time at the agreed-upon price. If the dealer does not exercise the option, the option payment is forfeited.

See Part II, Resources, for legal guidelines for handling some of these situations.

ORGANIZATION AND OUTLOOK

He who chooses the beginning of a road chooses the place it leads to. It is the means that determines the end.
— Harry Emerson Fosdick

One of the major organizational decisions facing the new dealer is whether to go it alone or with a partner, or perhaps with more than one partner. Many start out automatically as a team; for example, a couple seeking to extend their personal relationship into a business venture or friends who feel they would work well together. There's a lot to be said for having a partner in a business that requires you to spend as much time and effort in buying as in selling. In a retail store, partners can spell each other; in show situations, being alone is often just too physically exhausting. Most important, partners share expenses as well as work, and if well matched, each will bring particular strengths to the business.

The lone dealer can, of course, hire help or, at least at the beginning, work out an informal barter or consignment arrangement, the way Laura Fisher did. Another possibility is to have a loose partnership, where each dealer maintains separate records and inventory, but where expenses and labor are shared at show booths. Even a store can be shared on a cooperative basis, as will be seen in the next chapter.

If you are undecided or want further information about different types of business structures, the Small Business Administration, Washington, D.C. 20416, has a booklet (MA231) entitled *Selecting Legal Structure for Your Firm*, which discusses single proprietorships, partnerships, and incorporation. The Farmer's Cooperative Service of the U.S. Department of Agriculture has available several free publications explaining cooperative organization.

Once you've settled on a particular organizational structure, set down the details in your business plan notebook. Formal partnerships and incorporations should be handled by a lawyer. Even in an informal partnership arrangement (and I've run into a remarkable number of "handshake" situations in which considerable capital was at stake), it's best to spell out everything on paper. It is no reflection on your friendship, your marriage, or your mutual trust and respect to list details about responsibilities, possible dissolution of the partnership, or expenses. The whole purpose of writing things down, the essence of any legal agreement, is to avoid and not to cause future problems. As one partner in a three-way dealership told me: "At first we just jotted down a few simple rules about work and

financial responsibilities. We were sure that even this was too much
. . . but now, three years later, we find ourselves sitting down once
a month with new rules. It's not that we're not getting along, but the
rules help us to cope with new decisions that have accompanied
growth. They keep disagreements right out front, where they can be
resolved."

In addition to the personnel organization of your business, you
must also decide on the sales structure. Given the nature of the
merchandise you plan to sell, the nature and location of potential
customers, your personal lifestyle and finances, you will have to
make choices about the way you will conduct your dealership. Like
many, you may find your answer in a combination — shop owner
and a show dealer or show and mail order dealer, for example. Furthermore, an ancillary career may serve to enliven and enrich your
activities as a dealer. This book, it is hoped, will help you focus on
the right single effort or combination of efforts.

A Name to Formalize and Identify the Business

A name puts an official stamp on your plan of business. Without
a name you can't register your business, print up cards or stationery,
or make up signs. Think of your long-range plans, to avoid choosing
a name you may outgrow. If you have a particular specialty, can you
be sure that you won't branch out into other areas where a given
name may no longer convey what you are all about? Naming a shop
after the street where it is located will present problems of identification should you move to another location. If you use a made-up
name, you will have to obtain a certificate for doing business under
an assumed name; this involves a modest fee. You can combine a
word or phrase with your own name — Dan Smith's Past and Present Pleasures — and avoid this procedure.

There's a lot to be said for using your own name, either alone or in
combination with another word or words; it gives a sense of personal
involvement, integrity, and long-term purpose. A more general or a
catchy name has its own advantages, particularly for dealers in collectibles or items of nostalgia. However, catchy need not mean junk,
and I believe a name like Junktiques, though it may be accurately
descriptive of merchandise handled, is a declaration of low horizons.

Check out both your titles and slogans carefully before printing up a thousand cards, to make sure they are not used by others. At least four different dealers told me of plans for a truly drop-dead, one-of-a-kind card, which is to read "We Buy Junk" on one side and "We Sell Antiques" on the other. Maybe this will work for all of them, but it's best to be aware.

Following are some dealers' recollections about how they settled on made-up names that have worked well for them.

Betty Richman and Fran Schmidt, of Flushing, New York:

"We were sitting around, trying to figure out a name that would associate us with glass, since we sell so much of that, but which would also be catchy enough to be remembered by our mail order customers. A friend who dropped in ended our debate by announcing, 'Betty is the Rich Man, so Fran must be the Poor Man . . . Why not Rich Man, Poor Man?' Why not indeed? It was perfect!"

Hope Peek and Jackie Oosthuizen, of Constantia Antiques, Greenwich, Connecticut:

"Constantia is a name chosen unanimously, by us and our husbands, from a list of suggestions. It's a Dutch word, meaning constancy, and Jackie, who's of Dutch descent, suggested it. We all agreed that it had a gracious look and sound, and we liked the idea that it has been used for a long time as a name for females, great houses, and villages. It seemed further fitting in connection with Greenwich, because during the period of early settlement the area was for several years part of the Dutch colony of New Amsterdam."

Joe Stamps, of Funchies, Bunkers, Gaks and Gleeks, Manhattan Art and Antiques Center, New York City:

"I had gone to an auction at Parke Bernet's PB Eighty-Four annex, and when the bidding was over I was flabbergasted at being presented with a bill for three thousand dollars. It turned out that there were two other guys named Stamps at that auction, and it took us quite a while to sort out our bills. Right then I made up my mind to create a name that would be so difficult that I'd never run into a double again . . . and so, Funchies, Bunkers, Gaks and Gleeks."

This is rather a perfect name for Joe, since it epitomizes his own whimsical charm as well as the mixture of marvels he carries in his shop. There is a postscript to Joe's original name choice, though. Very shortly after the new name was mounted in the window of the shop, two fellows came by, and Joe heard one say to the other, "Oh, s——t, I thought we had that name copyrighted!" So much for anything under the sun being unique!

Looking Ahead

Looking ahead to and striving for some particular satisfaction is essential to a pleasurable and meaningful life. Try to project your goals for the next five years. Perhaps some sample projections by others will help you to summarize your own:

1. "When I first decided to become a dealer, I knew that I wanted to do something that I enjoyed which would take me away from my home and family, but still not cut too deeply into that part of my life. I want to learn and do new things and be in contact with people who share my interests. I love antiques and want to have an excuse to buy beyond personal collecting. I want to have all this add up to a profit. Eventually, I want to travel more, buy more, and definitely make more money. I consider profit more important to the long-range than the short-range goal."

2. "I've had a career in industry and made a lot of money. I want something more direct, which allows me to say 'This is mine — I built it.' My other career centered on plastics, and now I want to be involved in products that have an esthetic and not just a functional appeal. I do not want to trade the profit motive for subsistence income, though I'm willing to start out making a lot less than I was making. In other words, I'm willing to tighten my belt for a couple of years and lower my eventual dollar horizons somewhat from what they were, but my five-year plan definitely includes profit in the comfortable regions of a five-figure income."

Both of the statements above contain short-term and long-term goals. The first stage of the plan covers the period in which you get going and work to survive. If you make it through, a growth period follows. Each plan calls for a different strategy. The first dealer has to achieve goals within the boundaries of the personal situation she wants to maintain. The second dealer is obviously freer to pursue the stated plan full steam ahead, with the likelihood of a better capital foundation from the previous career.

Your plan may entail its own strictures, and the long range may strike you as too far away to be real. Write it down anyway. You can always change it. You most likely will. Even if you are a retiree, think about your children or grandchildren. Your long-range plans can incorporate the likelihood of their wanting to take over what you've begun.

Whatever the eventual pattern of your business, by setting down long-range goals you give yourself a better chance to exercise all possible options.

CHAPTER 2

❖ ❖ ❖

Today's Dealer . . .
Traditional Roles

The enormous growth of the antiques-collectibles market and the accompanying increase in the number of sellers vying for the collector's dollars have also enlarged and diversified the dealer's role. Because the modern dealer rarely fits a single, neat classification, Chapter 3 will be essentially a continuation of this one. Each dealer tends to winnow what best suits his needs from the more general classifications.

DEALER'S AGENT, OR "PICKER"

I first heard the word "picker" during a visit to my friends Florence and John Cummins, in Laconia, New Hampshire, some fifteen years ago. We'd met in New York, where they lived in a tiny apartment with two babies and a dog, but nary an antique in sight. Their New Hampshire house was brimful of interesting furniture, bric-a-brac, and other curiosities. As I admiringly examined everything, John announced, "Yes, been doing a little pickin'."

At one time a picker was able literally to pick up things left in and around abandoned houses, or from the town dump. He could knock on someone's door (thus the alternate term, knocker) asking if the owner had anything she wanted to be rid of. Often the knock brought a load of treasures. Even if the picker paid for them, the prices were not much higher than "for free."

Today many town dumps have turned into well-stocked thrift shops, and people are less wont to give away their old things; instead, they tend to invest them with exaggerated value. As a result, the picker has to run around more and farther and be cleverer and cleverer in tracking down bargains. Instead of simply knocking on doors, the picker now places ads in local papers to reach private sellers. Connections are established, if not with bankers and lawyers, then with plumbers and painters and others who have access to buildings where the buys may be.

Basically, all dealers are pickers, too, except that they must pare down the potential picking places to those most likely to be fruitful, and depend on the picker to attend small auctions and out-of-the-way church and house sales. The progression from picker-collector to picker-for-other-dealers to dealer is very common. My friend John today has an antique shop in the town of Franklin. Other pickers take their wares directly to the consumer by way of flea markets and shows. Some stockpile their pickings and sell them through mail order catalogues. According to Jack Lawton Webb, who writes a column, Market Trends, for *Antique & Collectors' Mart*, the traveling picker seems more and more to have reversed roles with the dealer he once supplied — so more often than not it is the traveling dealer who visits the local picker in his shop!

Many stay with picking for other dealers and auctioneers for a long time, but instead of buying at random they go out with specific orders from dealers, who often advance the money for the purchase and guarantee a commission on delivery. I met several people who were actually paid employees of large secondhand and wholesale antiques sales galleries, with vacations and all the legal benefits of a "real job." There is yet another term often used to describe the picker: the hauler. This semantic distinction is made for the picker who travels with a van or truck and hauls loads of merchandise to a dealer's or auctioneer's warehouse.

A Couple Who "Picked" Their Way to a Dealership

Sonja and Victor Farber's first exposure to anything resembling antiques or antiques dealings occurred when a sister-in-law, whose home had a lot of nice things, decided to change her décor and sell off some of her old furnishings to friends and relatives.

"That was way before garage sales and the idea of collecting antiques took hold for people with our kind of poor, cultureless backgrounds," Sonja recalled. "We felt obligated to go, and went with our minds made up to buy the cheapest thing there, which turned out to be a fifty-cent English pitcher. Cheap or not, it was lovely."

That purchase marked several years of rather haphazard, always inexpensive collecting, mostly in out-of-the-way junk shops and church bazaars. Then the same sister-in-law who had sold them the original pitcher, and who now came around regularly to admire their newest finds, introduced them to a local dealer whose wares they had never been able to afford. The dealer suggested that they buy things with the idea of reselling them to her.

And so the Farbers became pickers. They knew as little about pricing as they once did about antiques, but in their price range it seemed automatic just to mark everything double the cost. When they moved to Connecticut, their buying forays increased to the point where their original dealer no longer had room for all they bought. She encouraged them to try other dealers, and soon the Farbers found themselves with a whole group of dealers, right in Connecticut, happy to buy everything they brought. Their next move, from picking to direct retailing, was once again initiated by their sister-in-law, who was spending the summer in a nearby resort hotel where "antiquing" had begun to be a form of recreation. She told the other guests, "You haven't seen good buys until you've seen what my sister-in-law and brother-in-law buy. They sell to dealers!" The hotel guests naturally did want to see, and they ended up buying everything in the Farbers' house. It was at this point that five years as picker-collectors and then pickers-for-dealers came to an end.

From Pickers to At-Home Dealers

When Sonja and Victor Farber decided to open a shop, they

planned it as a full-time venture for Sonja, with Victor keeping his job as a carpenter. In fact, their move to Lynbrook, Long Island, was the result of his obtaining a new job in that town. The Farbers put a want ad in the papers, stating their need for a store, and an astute real estate agent suggested a property that, though located in a business zone, provided suitable living quarters. In the ensuing seventeen years, many additions have been made to the original building. Though the shop requires visitors to pick their way through a jumble of disarray, in old-style antique shop tradition, the upstairs apartment is a neat and charming example of how to live with antiques.

The Farbers' location is not exactly in the hub of antiques-buying activity. However, there is enough buying and selling throughout the Long Island area, and the Farbers' reputation has become sufficiently established, so that people seek them out from as far away as Massachusetts and Tennessee. They, in turn, continue to buy wherever they can, though they have been able to buy out many houses and shops within ready distance. Although Victor has long since quit his job as carpenter, his crafts skills have contributed vastly to the success of the business. He can buy things that need repair and also make use of nonvaluable items for parts. Their card reads very simply "Farber, Sonja and Victor." A descriptive subheading shows that they have stayed true to their original inclinations: "Antiques and Accessories . . . Off-Beat Items at Reasonable Prices."

Asked to explain their longevity in the business, Victor Farber says, without hesitation, "An instinct for buying . . . my being handy and thus able to profit from purchases which would be meaningless to others . . . and the confidence to keep buying and spend *thousands* whenever things are available, even if business is slow."

Though the wealthy private and business collector's acceptance and support of antiques as good investment have no doubt rubbed off on buyers of more modest means, Victor feels that investment is not really the basic motivation of his customers. He consequently considers the stability of the general economy vital to the good health of his kind of enterprise, the sale of merchandise for gifts and personal use, and sees recessionary periods as much more threatening than the competition from proliferating flea markets, which many other dealers denounce.

ATTIC DEALERS

The attic dealer is one who sells from home, but without any kind of a shop sign. Customers come by appointment only and through word-of-mouth recommendations. Customer traffic is usually no heavier than the flow in and out of any private home. Nevertheless, some very successful and long-established dealers have managed to keep inventories regularly and profitably turned by virtue of their reputation with a few selected dealer-customers.

Many attic dealers are primarily hobbyists who are not quite sure if and how they can turn their avocation into a vocation. Linda and Robert Malkin, for example, have amassed a large collection of out-sized commercial trade objects. At this point most of their collecting is for personal pleasure but since Linda is an interior decorator (an excellent background and second career, especially for anyone dealing with decorative objects), some items of the collection are sold to Linda's clients and to other decorators.

Some of the oversized commercial collectibles in Linda and Bob Malkin's attic shop.

It's always a sound idea to check local zoning regulations before doing any sort of selling from home. Some neighborhoods have very strict home business regulations while others issue variances if the selling does not include a sign or bring undue traffic.

Hanging Out a Sign in Front of Your Home

If your home is in an area without any sort of restrictions on business, you may want to hang out a sign and have the best of all worlds — a regular shop, right in your own home. The at-home shop situation holds much appeal. One of the major expenses, rent, is one you would be meeting anyway, and you will actually be able to deduct from your taxable income that portion of your home used for business. Before you count that as earnings, however, keep in mind that any improvements or alterations cost money and can result in an increased tax assessment on your entire property. Combining home and business also calls for the cooperation, support, and interest of family members, so the emotional and personal factors must be weighed against the financial pluses.

An At-Home Shop to Utilize Existing Space

Sometimes the idea of opening a shop is actually born from a desire to utilize a good, heretofore unused space. A barn and ice house sitting idly on the property of the Dautrich family of Goshen, Connecticut, are a case in point. Once the idea of an antique shop took hold, Jeanne Dautrich spent six weeks taking an intensive and all-inclusive course in antiques with the Morrises of Stamford, Connecticut; visiting museums and historical societies; attending good antiques shows; and reading, reading, reading! Within a year, Tranquil Acres Antiques was on sound footing as a middle-income business that occupies its owner with keeping shop from April through December, and buying for the following season from January until reopening.

Jeanne credits much of her success to the good fortune of having access to three types of professionals considered important contacts in the antiques business. She's married to a doctor; she used to work for a lawyer; and she's the mother of a realtor. Many of Dr. Dautrich's patients buy from and sell to Jeanne, and because she is privy to estate and house sale "scoops," she has acquired an inventory and clientele that more than offset any disadvantage which might otherwise accompany her shop's being on a private dead-end road. Insurance agents, and yes, even funeral directors, are some equally advantageous connections for a budding dealer.

Here are some of Jeanne Dautrich's business precepts for giving a boost to good fortune:

1. Make a sound investment. Jeanne feels anyone starting with as little as $5000 should work it up as much as possible. She considers

Jeanne Dautrich, Tranquil Acres Antiques

$50,000 a really sound start-up — with continual reinvestment.

2. Quantity and diversity of merchandise bought in large lots has worked best for her. She believes that a chance to purchase an entire barn lot and then an antique dealer's complete house gave her the good start that set her on the road to almost immediate earnings.

3. Take advantage of the gift potential of nice decorative accessories, such as thin china cups and saucers, as well as specific collectibles like miniature shoes, salt shakers, and spoons. A good selection of fast-turnover items like this give bread-and-butter solidity to larger things.

4. Stick to the put-and-sell principle of buying. In other words, don't make an offer if you can avoid it, but let the seller name the price. If the price is too high to permit a 50 percent markup, let it go.

5. Don't just sit with "mistakes" or things bought as part of a large lot. If you feel something will move eventually, take it out of inventory for a while so that the store has a fresh look. Otherwise, turn a low markup or even a loss to your promotional advantage. Jeanne, for example, runs the annual Tranquil Acres Tag Sale, which gets rid of a lot of "mistakes" and has become something of an anticipated institution with customers.

6. Merchandise should be well displayed and clean, to attract people who buy antiques and collectibles. Jeanne concentrates on merchandise in good condition and spends much time polishing.

7. Treat each customer as an important one. Jeanne has had youngsters buying small items "on account" and makes them feel as welcome as larger cash buyers. New and regular customers receive a reopening notice each April, with a personally penned note, such as "Hope you're enjoying the chest." Information for these notes is taken from check receipts and a carefully maintained guest log.

If you don't have Jeanne Dautrich's good connections, keep in mind some of these pickers' methods for making contacts: Put up signs about your buying interests in supermarkets, store windows, and other places with bulletin boards. Go to each and every garage and tag sale you see listed, and get there early, with a list of things to *ask* for. For certain kinds of things, like quilts, consider advertising your interest with classified ads, not just in your own local paper, but in locals a great distance away. (See *Ayer Directory*, listed in In-

Print Information, Part II, Resources, to find out about media and geographic demography.)

AWAY-FROM-HOME SHOPS

Even if there are no legal deterrents to your opening a shop at home, the location or the house itself may be unsuitable. You can either move or opt for a separate shop. The appearance of the shop, the customer's ability to envision immediately how something will look at home, clearly tagged prices instead of coded ones — all these can mean the difference between an active, going concern and one that is just hanging in there. No matter how good your location, expect to expend at least some of your effort in going out to where the buyers are.

Antiques: A Joint Venture

Meg and Bruce Cummings of Hadley, Massachusetts, typify today's new dealers. They are young, attractive, and well educated. Bruce knew even before he graduated from the University of Massachusetts that being a physicist was not for him, but Meg actually practiced her originally planned profession as an elementary school teacher for two and a half years.

It was while attending the university that Bruce found himself drawn to the Saturday morning sales at the Amherst Auction Galleries. After he bought a stamp collection and began to sell off parts of it, the whole process got him hooked on buying and selling. By the time he and Meg got married five years ago, he was a dealer, she was teaching, and on weekends they ran the food concession at the Amherst Auction Galleries. What they lacked in capital they amply compensated for in energy.

The Cummings' shop, on a very well-traveled road in Hadley, is the same one Bruce started out in, except that at first it was run as a sort of mall-within-a-shop. The cost of rent and heat and electricity was shared by three other young dealers, and the 600 feet of space were divided into four individual booths. It worked out well in terms of cooperation among the cotenants and served much the same purpose as Laura Fisher's test period in her auctioned space at a New York center. However, everyone except Bruce chose other ways and places, so he and Meg decided they would carry the store together.

Since the shop became a venture for two, it has enjoyed steady growth. A very sizable inventory, with emphasis on oak furniture, nonetheless leaves the visitor with plenty of room to move around. Displays are attractively grouped, and everything is as it will be in someone's home. The Cummings recently broke through the rear of their store and into the back of the one next door, thus doubling their space.

Like many furniture dealers, Meg and Bruce find refinishing (no stripping, though) helps them to increase profits and achieve the antique "showroom" look that seems to sell well. In true joint-venture fashion, Meg took a course in caning; she usually has a chair going. This works as an in-store demonstration and is very good for business. If someone asks what she's doing, she tells him, to his delight, that if he buys the chair, he can have it with the caning thrown in, at no extra cost.

Although both Meg and Bruce radiate enthusiasm and optimism, and certainly seem well past the failure-prone period predicted for most new businesses, they neither keep the hours nor earn the income they would have had if he had become a physicist and she had remained in education. They work hard in the shop and out, because, obviously, a turning inventory must always be replaced. During the weekend I spent in Amherst, Bruce went to the Saturday morning auction at the Amherst Auction Galleries, spent time in the shop with Meg, and later that evening they both attended Mark Polon's auction (see Chapter 5) in nearby Greenfield. On Sunday morning they were lined up to shop their way through the annual antiques flea market at Amherst College's Cage.

When I asked Bruce about some of his best buys, it became clear that this was the part of the business that brought him the most satisfaction. "A really super buy is not so much something obtained for twenty dollars or even a hundred dollars and then sold for nine or ten times that. Anybody can do that," he explained, "since there isn't any risk. No, to me the real best buy is the one where I spend a thousand dollars for something and sell it for three thousand. That way you have a nice profit, but you also have the satisfaction of knowing you had the savvy and the sense to take a risk."

Colby Antiques

The two shops currently operating under the umbrella title of Colby Antiques are about the same age as Antiques: A Joint Venture. However, Mary Colby's arrival on the antiques scene in San Clemente, California, was preceded by forty years of experience in the

Meg and Bruce Cummings in their shop, Antiques: A Joint Venture.

business. The shops were started as a retirement venture, a highly condensed, strictly antiques version of a chain of fine import shops.

For someone with Mary Colby's energy and acumen, it has been impossible to contain growth within the usual concept of "retirement" activity; therefore the two shops rather than one, a large warehouse, and a half-dozen employees. Her previous enterprise and the invaluable experience gained as European antiques buyer for a large American department store right after World War II added up to the sort of experience and reserve capital a younger dealer would have had to acquire step by step. Mrs. Colby is optimistic about the opportunities for young people who want to get into the business, if they are willing to go the apprenticeship route. "I do not believe that working in a department store, as I did, is the best way to learn the trade today. Times have changed," she says.

Assistants working for her to learn the business have to start at the minimum wage, but they have access to her vast library of books and periodicals, many of them very expensive. Of the nineteen publications to which she subscribes, she cites the English *Collector's Guide* and the American magazine *Antiques* as important for antiques taste trends; the *Art-Antiques Investment Review* and *International Art Market* best for business information about antiques and pictures; and for keeping abreast generally of upper-echelon clientele tastes, she considers *Architectural Digest* her best help. See Part II, Resources, for details on these publications.

CHAPTER 3

❖ ❖ ❖

The Dealer's
Modus Operandi
Expands

The restoration activities that serve as "extras" for many shops like Antiques: A Joint Venture, described in the last chapter, can be full-time ventures in and of themselves, as you will see in Chapter 6. There are many other ways of building traffic and defraying costs.

Jo Ann and Al Peselnick, who run a shop in Floral Park, New York, have developed a videotape inventory service, for collectors and home owners who want an audio-visual record of their belongings that will stand up in court in the event of an insurance claim. This represents a rather costly investment. However, those with a bent for photography may consider a much more modified service for customers who want a slide or black-and-white print record of their possessions for their pleasure as much as for insurance purposes. To take this a step farther, photographs of a dealer's own sold items, with prices carefully recorded, may add up to a potential price guide, which can then be reproduced and used as a for-sale extra or promotional give-away, for customers or other dealers.

Some dealers in resort towns have successfully expanded the concept of living over or next door to their shops. They have setups that allow potential customers, too, to live near the shops. The business card of Victor Caffese and Peter Winn, of Ogunquit, Maine, describes their Spendid Era Antiques shop on one side, their Yellow Monkey guesthouse on the other. This combination is also suitable for those dealers who rely on shows for off-season income, since the antiques and tourist seasons coincide.

The antique shop that doubles as an interior design studio or consultation service is another happy and satisfying combination. For Christie Donoghue, the arrangement helped her establish a new European antiques business after she left her native Germany to marry a Texan. Bill Donoghue found the antiques trade more interesting than his own activities and became Christie's business partner. Their large showcase building in Victoria blends shop and home. They also have formed excellent contacts with Houston buyers, through that city's prestigious Theta Show.

In spite of Christie's European connections, she and Bill do all their buying from New York auctioneers and import wholesalers: "We prefer to let the big importers bring in the pudding; then we buy the raisins from them." They caution newcomers against jumping into overseas buying as well as into large expensive imports.

The Donoghues were not the only dealers to discourage others from buying abroad. The process entails too many costs in addition to the price rises resulting from extensive back-and-forth, rather than just import, trading. As one dealer put it, "Certain furniture has crossed the ocean more times than Jacqueline Onassis!"

In spite of these caveats, the lure of traveling, if not bargains, will always induce people to buy abroad. In fact, even those who warn against expecting enormous bargains when shopping abroad, do admit to the advantages of combining business with pleasure. As one man said, "If you're going to take a trip anyway, naturally, you're going to at least look around for merchandise."

At times, the interior decorating business precedes the antiques business. A case in point is Conway Antiques and Décor in Rutland, Vermont, operated by Thomas Conway and Thomas Brown. The business was started by Mr. Conway's mother, an interior designer, twenty-three years ago and has blossomed into a combination enterprise under her son's management.

CLUSTERING: THE MALL EXPERIENCE

Experienced dealers have long recognized the value of being located amid or at least near a whole clutch of shops in order to attract the customer to whom antiquing represents a day or a weekend of buying. Resort towns, travel books, organized tours, all cater to the recreational aspects of antiquing, and dealers have learned that just as many a collector is a dealer in the making, so a browser is indeed a potential buyer! Being the only dealer in town, far from being an advantage, is a distinct disadvantage in terms of attracting the browser-buyer. This has encouraged the idea of dealers concentrating shops in one village street or in especially enclosed malls and buildings. The mall concept has been implemented throughout the country — in fact, the world — with many variations to the basic theme.

Christie and Bill Donoghue's European antiques and interior design business is housed in an impressive building in Victoria, Texas. The building is also the Donoghue's home, with a separate entrance.

Visitors to the Donoghues' shop see objets d'art as they would fit into their own interior spaces.

There are large multishop malls and small six-to-ten-shop setups — some devoted strictly to antiques, some to antiques and collectibles, some to antiques and crafts, some to antiques as giftware, and so on. Physical layouts range from shops and booths with locked doors or gates to open displays that don't have to be attended by the owners at all. Individuals can get together to subdivide large shops or houses, either selling on a cooperative basis, or maintaining separate records. One room can be set aside as a showcase for all.

Safety is one of the chief reasons many dealers have chosen to go into malls, even at the risk of losing a certain amount of street traffic. Companionship is another. For the newcomer, a small space can offer a relatively low-cost opportunity to be in an area otherwise unaffordable, to enjoy the benefits of being registered with tourist and travel centers (an expense borne by the good mall manager). In large cities, the malls tend to attract television and magazine stylists looking for a central source for rentals of antiques as backdrops. (See Rental Agreement under Legal Matters in Part II, Resources.)

The Mall Experience: Eastern, Southern, and Midwestern Style

Joe Stamps' shop may not be the largest in the Manhattan Art and Antiques Center, but it probably boasts the longest name, as well as one of the more eclectic mixtures of antiques and collectibles in the entire three-level structure. Funchies, Bunkers, Gaks and Gleeks reflects the sparkling wit that guided its owner up the ladder in his earlier career in advertising. Like his neighbor, Laura Fisher (see Chapter 1), Joe began his life as a dealer in another center. He moved to the current site because it offers a "real shop with a door," an *on*-the-avenue (Second Avenue, between Fifty-fifth and Fifty-sixth streets) rather than *off*-the-avenue location. The choice of the mall rather than a single shop facing the street was based on economics and safety in fairly equal order of importance. The choice of a somewhat back-of-the-bus location within the mall was strictly economic, since Joe still considers himself very much the new boy in town. This, in turn, has motivated him to reactivate his dormant advertising and promotional skills to write a column, headed with the shop's name. His irreverent but rarely irrelevant column, published every month in the *New York Antiques Almanac*, provides him with a bit of

When an advertising man becomes an antiques dealer, his old skills don't just fade away. This is my all-time favorite Joe Stamps ad.

extra income and free advertising. Though Joe is currently concentrating on making the shop a major success, he could undoubtedly extend his career in antiques to developing ads for other dealers interested in creating some really memorable spots or campaigns.

The eclecticism of the Funchies, Bunkers, Gaks and Gleeks' inventory, as opposed to the carefully planned concentration on primitive Americana in Laura Fisher's shop, is a direct result of the rather unfocused auction fever that propelled Joe into dealing to begin

Joe Stamps — also known as Funchies, Bunkers, Gaks and Gleeks — surrounded by some of his favorite antiquities.

with. If there is one area in which he would eventually like to specialize, it is Renaissance furniture. Right now, by virtue of the mall's space perimeters, this must remain in the Funchies' "annex," the large treasure-packed apartment Joe shares with his friend and part-time partner, Al Peacock, and five cats.

As Joe Stamps is one of the newer boys in the Manhattan Antiques Center, so Mel Nash is one of the newer girls in her town of Winston-Salem, North Carolina, in a mall known as the Old Salem Home and Antiques Galleries. Mel and her husband, Richard, furnished their home with fine antique furniture and accessories, and in the process she found that her interest extended beyond personal belongings. When Mel decided to go into business she chose, for a number of reasons, a booth in the Old Salem mall rather than a shop of her own:

1. The mall, located at the north end of Old Salem, has been integrated into the restored village as a major tourist attraction.

2. The reconverted building's large and attractive floor-through space made for an attractive mini-mall setting. Booths, though small (100 to 300 square feet), offered good rental value at an average of $5.50 per square foot per annum, paid on a monthly basis.

3. With two managers to handle all sales, at a commission of 10 percent, dealers are not confined to retail selling — though they are free to come in to stock, rearrange merchandise, and talk to customers.

4. The fact that the mall has other attractions for visitors serves to increase traffic for everyone. The main floor holds the new and reproduction furniture of Leland De Blake, who converted and owns the building; the basement is a consignment shop for antiques and collectibles bargain-seekers.

Many dealers who have regular shops elsewhere also rent booths in the Old Salem Antiques Galleries — somewhat like showroom annexes. This is an option Mel may exercise eventually, though she has found the mall setup alone an ideal and relaxed way to ease into the business, to be able to buy frequently both locally and in other parts of the country and in England. The fact that the merchandise in her booth changes every month is testimony to the astuteness of her buying.

In spite of such encouraging initial success, she is always on the lookout for ways to improve her sales and cut down expenses. For example, she takes in needlepoint pillows by local artists for a 10 percent commission. The pillows enhance her displays and the commission gives her a small additional profit. To add to the appeal of her best sellers, hanging cupboards and shelves, she stocks a special seasoned salt, which she buys wholesale from a small manufacturer in Florida, as a gift item. (See Chapter 8, Spinoffs.) Twice a year she takes a space at a large local antiques show. This not only results in good immediate sales, but brings spinoff business to her mall booth.

Not every dealer is willing to give up control over his or her merchandise, even for the consequent freedom. The decision is a personal one, and the results depend very much on finding a mall that

Mel Nash's booth at the Old Salem Home and Antiques Galleries is a small, open space. The inventory changes every month.

maintains high quality and has good management, run with integrity and cooperation among all involved.

Fjelde & Co., Antiques, in Minneapolis is a shop complex that has grown from one converted old building, at the corner of Fiftieth and Xerxer Avenue in the southern section of the city, into a whole network of independent stores that has made "the corner" a mecca for antiques buyers. The man who began it all, Rick Fjelde, had a background in architecture and a love of antiques. He and his wife, Jenny, were interested, as well, in the idea of resale. When Rick came into some money, he decided to buy an old structure, and convert it into an antique center. Several shops, two of which still existed, had previously been housed in the area, and he felt this association with antiques offered a distinct advantage. In spite of the

Here is an overview of the Old Salem mall space. Photographer, Cooky Snyder

additional capital of a silent partner, the Fjeldes' ideas for remodeling and acquiring adjoining space far exceeded their funds. As a consequence, they took in a number of other people and became a cooperative. When the Fjeldes moved to Illinois some years later, one of the co-op members, Ralph Popehn, a journalism graduate from the University of Minnesota, took over the management of the Fjeldes' own large space within the complex.

Currently there are eight cooperating partners in the Fjelde & Co. building. The space allocation is quite different from other malls. Instead of specific, permanently located spaces, Fjelde partners are entitled to a set amount of space for display of merchandise, but the location of their space is not permanent. This makes it possible to have an overall arrangement resembling one big country store, with areas and rooms periodically set aside for particular types of merchandise. Each partner has a chance to place merchandise within an appropriate area and according to Mrs. Margaret Scholer, a local expert and lecturer who has been associated with "the corner" in some way for the last ten years, it has all worked very well "because each participant has been very honorable in using the allocated amounts of space for the general good." She also cites the flexibility in organizational rules. For example, though individuals may trade off their work days in the shop, there is a group-planned schedule posted weekly. If someone comes in to sell merchandise or offer a whole house, it is the person on duty who has the right to refuse or to buy. There is also a subsidiary co-op of members who do restoration. If any of the cooperators sell at shows, they do so under the corporate name. On occasion the co-op meetings are enlarged to include all the tenants of the complex of shops that extended from the original building.

WHEELING AND DEALING: THE SHOW DEALER

From the preceding sampling of at-home and away-from-home dealerships, it would seem that the antique shop continues to be a viable part of the retail trade. However, the picture that emerges is one of more shops emphasizing modern merchandising techniques in site selection, interior display, and personal selling. What is most significant is that very few dealers stay put in their shops. In addition to buying aggressively, instead of waiting for people to bring things into the shop, dealers go to where the market is.

The show — from flea market to highest-quality, regularly scheduled, prestige event — is an indisputable and vital reality for anyone dealing in antiques or collectibles. For countless numbers, the show has become *the* market outlet, a permanent way of setting up impermanent shops. The shows are selected on the basis of promoter's reputation, the dealer's desired itinerary, and type of inventory. Merchandise is often bought and specially earmarked for particular types of shows. Dealers at flea markets frequently have more or less permanent sites, so in addition to casual mass-market traffic, they cater to regular customers, who know where to find them and when.

Announcements of shows can be found in the antiques pages of general newspapers or in antiques publications. Since selection can be mind-boggling, it's best to obtain word-of-mouth advice either from a friend or by visiting shows and asking questions of exhibiting dealers. Your decisions will depend on your ability and willingness to travel, as well as the type of merchandise sold.

As for estimated earnings, hard-and-fast figures are nonexistent. Many dealers judge earnings according to this rule of thumb: you should earn six times the cost of the booth. Generally agreed-upon rock-bottom earnings fall in the $200-to-$400 range. In spite of dealers' complaints about too many shows, enough of them continue to sign up for twenty or more a year to indicate that earnings are not on the lower end of the scale.

Bruce Blank traded his career as a pharmacist for one as a shop and show dealer "when I saw fifty thousand dollars and sixty thousand dollars in college tuition looming ahead." He feels that the description of the antiques business as a nonearning one is a myth. He sells fine bronzes, Orientalia, and European antiques at ten or more large shows annually, and has created a flea market flavor in his Valley Stream, Long Island, shop, Horse's Head Antiques. Shows and shops, plus European vacation–buying trips, are kept in balance with the help of his wife, Harriet, and hired help in the shop.

Show Stoppers

With show visitors often overwhelmed by an overabundance of treasures, many experienced dealers have learned to bring pieces that really stand out at a show. Some also get into the spirit of things by wearing clothing in keeping with the period that is being evoked.

Some Second-Career Show Dealers

Ray and Lee Grover, of Ohio and Florida, have brought the kind of expertise, business organization, flair, and money to their dealership in fine glass that would have made them the likely proprietors of a large museumlike emporium, in the manner of La Vieille Russie on New York's Fifth Avenue, had they gone into the business forty

This all-silver miniature room may not find a buyer, since its price tag is quite high, but it's a sure-fire show stopper for miniature and silver enthusiasts.

years ago instead of twenty. Since Ray concentrated his first career in the building supply business, the Grovers turned their long-standing love affair with fine glass into another business, but on a controlled-time basis, which led to the decision to do shows only, exactly ten a year. Although they have controlled their time involvement, everything the Grovers do is on a grand and important scale — their booths are usually triple-sized, with numerous rented, locked cases in which their wares are displayed and labeled, as in a museum. Shows are carefully scheduled and chosen according to the Grovers' own geographic preferences and the quality of the management. They announce their schedule by means of large ads in *Hobbies* magazine. They are personally in attendance at each show and main-

The Wooton desk is Eileen Dubrow's trademark, and she manages to take one to every show she does.

tain a year-round office with a full-time secretary in Cleveland, so that people who want to buy or sell can always contact them.

"Not having a store does not mean you don't have a high overhead," Ray Grover told me. Both he and Lee are well aware that the average young person starting out could not put up the kind of capital required to build their kind of inventory and operate on their level of expenditure.

Several handsomely illustrated books on fine glass have added yet another dimension to this enriching (in every way!) retirement career. A twenty-one-year-old grandson has expressed interest in continuing what they have built up.

When Nancy Greenberg takes her Antiques for Collectors, of Pipersville, Pennsylvania, to a show, she finds that getting into the spirit of things with an appropriate costume helps to put customers into the spirit also — to buy, that is.

For Jane MacNeil, proprietor of Holyport English Antiques, being a show dealer also marked the beginning of a second career, though her retirement from newspaper and television work was the consequence of motherhood rather than maturity. She's thirty-six. Her antiques passion was born when her husband, Robert MacNeil, was a reporter for the BBC. They bought a huge sixteenth-century barn to convert into a family home and furnish, when they could afford to do so, with antiques. The antiques passion took a serious professional turn some four years ago, when she took a stall at the Eton Antiques Market at Windsor, England.

By the time the MacNeils moved back to the States, to Bronxville, New York, Jane was a confirmed dealer, with a $20,000 inventory investment. With four children ranging from eighteen to seven, she found that a May-through-November show schedule in the New England area worked best for her. She may do as many as sixteen shows in that span. Until his fame as half of the "MacNeil/Lehrer Report" made him something of a sales detriment (people would talk current events instead of concentrating on buying), Robert used to come along and help out; now some of the children do. Unlike many dealers, who put buying ahead of selling, Jane MacNeil says, "I truly love selling to the collector who just has to have an item. I have made elaborate arrangements with several to help them accomplish it, and I seem to get very involved in other people's lives this way."

This involvement has also extended to friends who have been inspired by her to want to get into the business. She has launched four friends into the show circuit. Two of her protégées have become what she calls flea market junkies, captured more by the Damon Runyon flavor of the surroundings than by the objects themselves. One friend's aptitude as a student has become something of a mixed blessing; she is so successful that she and Jane now share containers for merchandise shipped in from abroad, and "we also compete for the same things." The fourth dropped out.

Jane herself, in spite of continuing enthusiasm for antiques, has become somewhat disillusioned with shows. She feels the consumer is being saturated with so many shows that it now takes two shows to sell what she once sold in one. "The costs have gone up, too. I don't expect every show to be spectacular, like the one where I sold two grandfather clocks and made six thousand dollars, but for a weekend show that costs two hundred dollars, I do feel one should come out somewhere near a thousand dollars."

SHOW-TO-DEALER TURNABOUTS

There are always some show dealers who, to ease the financial uncertainties, and the rigors of multishow life, decide to give the shop situation a try. Jane MacNeil decided to decrease her dependency on shows for income by forming a partnership in a consignment business with Patricia Silleck, long-time proprietor of one of the most successful antique shops in Greenwich, Connecticut. On Consignment charges 25 percent on consigned merchandise, including anything the two owners put in. In other words, if something belonging to Jane sells, Patricia charges 12½ percent.

Beryl Breen was a medical secretary for five years, real estate broker for seven, and banker for ten — with concurrent part-time show dealing. During a visit to her native England, she decided to build up her stock of estate silver and jewelry sufficiently to go into antiques on a full-time basis. She and her husband, Phil, a hardware executive who does fine furniture refinishing, determined to make a really drastic change, moving to a new house, with a shop, in a new place. They advertised in the widely circulated Connecticut paper the Newtown *Bee* for a house suitable for an antique shop. After about seven weeks they found just what they wanted, adjacent to the Deerfield Restoration in Massachusetts. To get themselves known in the Deerfield area, the Breens immediately took space in some local shows. They plan to continue selling at shows in other areas, except during the busiest tourist season.

SPECIALIZATION

I feel that specialization is almost a must if one plans to operate with any sort of integrity. Antiques is such a vast field, it would take several lifetimes to try to know everything.
— Stella Hall, Editor, *The Antiques Dealer*

The shop closest to being on the endangered species list is the one that carries an accumulated inventory of anything and everything, arranged without rhyme or reason. The psychology behind this is that the buyer, convinced that the dealer doesn't know what he's got and that countless treasures can be retrieved from the rubble, will willingly wind through the maze.

Beryl and Phil Breen in their at-home shop in Old Deerfield, Massachusetts, which they bought after years of being strictly show dealers.

The truth is that today's consumer is both educated and experienced enough to realize that forays into messy and disorganized places rarely yield much of anything, except dirty hands and clothing. There will always be some of these old curiosity shops to lure the incurable optimist, but on the whole the modern dealer, like the collector, tends to focus on specific interests enticingly displayed. Concentration still allows considerable leeway, from very specific and narrow to broader bases.

The Americana dealers carry everything from accessories to furniture, metal, and fibers; and even more narrow specialists will carry objects from a variety of periods. The specialists do buy large lots, in order to obtain the good things they want, which means that they, too, must know how to dispose of all sorts of merchandise. Sometimes this can be done quite simply, through tax deductible donations to charities and thrift shops or by consigning items to other dealers or to auctions.

Often specialization represents a way of dealing part-time, either as a self-apprenticeship while one holds down another job or as part of the winding-down process of semiretirement.

Two Part-Time Specialists

Herman Darvick's interest in collecting autographs began as a hobby, but it is far more than that today even though he has no immediate plans for giving up his career as an elementary school teacher. Darvick has been uncontested president of the United Autograph Collector's Club (Box 467, Rockville Centre, New York 11571) for ten years and edits that organization's newsletter. The club's regularly scheduled conventions and auctions, attended by members from all over the country, enable Herman to earn $8000 a year — a figure he feels he could easily double any time he decides to become a full-time dealer. His collecting, his close contacts with other dealers and collectors in the club, his astute buying, both by mail and at auctions like the Charles Hamilton autograph auctions in New York, have taken him well out of the hobbyist-dabbler class.

Herman also applies his collecting knowledge in the classroom and has introduced many youngsters not only to the historic lessons inherent in autograph collecting, but to the business aspects of collecting and dealing. At a Sunday afternoon show, held by the club, I saw two former students, now in high school, turn handsome profits as part of their first experience as paying exhibitors. President Darvick's on-the-spot guidance lent the sort of educational support and inspiration all too rare for those yearning for a sound, practical education in antiques — or anything!

R. B. Holm of Glouster, North Carolina, became a specialist by way of a general antique shop he used to run in Laguna Beach, California. "The women used to come in and the men waited in the car," Mr. Holm recalls, "so I started to put things I especially liked into a separate room — military items, nude paintings, and tools and other strong, rustic stuff. I'd tell the women to send the men in to see my little museum, and eventually this became more popular than the general stuff." Over the years, Mr. Holm has specialized in other things that have been successful for him. "You've got to smell a trend and follow up on it."

At this time Male Antiques are his one and only specialty, since he wants to spend more time fishing. He and his wife travel in a comfortable motor home to a number of large shows. He says the antiques business has been good to him and sees no obstacle to anyone's earning up to $20,000 a year; it's making the jump into the higher levels that he considers trickier. In addition to the shows, Male Antiques makes contact with buyers through mail order advertising — which brings us to the last of the methods used more and more frequently as either all or part of a dealer's operation.

SELLING BY MAIL

If your own neighborhood is not a good source of customers, or if the merchandise you want to sell is more valued in other parts of the country, mail order advertising will enable you to reach these otherwise unreachable customers. The advertising results not only in immediate contacts but in echo effects: good will and usable names for direct mail selling. Readers seeing the ad will often offer you items similar to what they've seen advertised, thus helping to replenish your inventory.

The following view of direct mail selling can also serve as a guide for those who want to use this method to buy. See Part II, Resources, for other types of advertising methods and guidelines.

Rich Man, Poor Man:
The Antique Trader Weekly *Is Their Shop*

To readers of the glass and china section of *The Antique Trader Weekly*, Betty Richman and Fran Schmidt are known as Rich Man, Poor Man, the firm name under which they have conducted a mail order business for more than four years. The business began, on even less than the proverbial shoestring, more as a lark than a planned, continuous profit venture. However, like most women who have interrupted business careers for domesticity and motherhood, Betty and Fran were ready to seize an opportunity for resuming a career.

To start at the beginning: the women are married to avid watch collectors, though it took the two noncollecting women (Betty did have a general long-standing interest in antiques) to bring the watch aficionados together. Once the "match" was made, according to Fran, "the love affair was on, and it was the last time we saw our husbands." At antiques shows and fairs, the men went off in pursuit of their interests while the women browsed around on their own.

Looking inevitably leads to buying, and buying in turn to reading up on things. After three or four years of this rather casual tag-along collecting, Betty and Fran came across a piece of china they felt had good resale value. They decided to split the cost of buying it and taking an ad to sell it. The Richmans had been subscribing to the *Trader* for years, so this was an automatic and, as it turned out, good choice. They reinvested the profit from that first sale, plus additional savings, and began to buy steadily for the specific purpose of reselling by mail.

What gives merchandise good advertising qualities? (1) It is readily identifiable, describable in words that evoke a clear image. (2) It's modestly to moderately priced, obtainable in the dealer's locale and desirable and rarer in some distant places where the ad will be read. As Betty puts it, "If Ohio left the Union, we would go out of business in New York." (3) It is relatively easy to ship.

The Rich Man, Poor Man ads have grown from single- to double-column five-inch ads. Occasionally, the firm advertises in *Hobbies,* which, like the *Trader,* attracts a lot of the Midwestern customers who have proven best for their kind of merchandise. Asked to cite some comments and suggestions based on their experiences, Betty and Fran offered the following list:

1. Don't expect checks and orders to roll in automatically. The Rich Man, Poor Man ads are very clear and specific, but as a rule people call or write for a picture. Since most of the responses come within a few days of an ad's appearance, you must be available to receive phone calls.

2. Advertising in a weekly paper allows you to reach a wide geographic market fast, but remember that the mail system is far from perfect. It's a good idea to put in a reminder, at least occasionally, that people should feel free to call even if their paper arrives late. Before you advertise in a monthly, be well aware of the time spread during which you have to tie up your inventory.

3. In order for mail order to be anything but a one-shot endeavor, ads must be evaluated and used with a long-range view. It's the rare ad that's a sellout; selling half of what you advertise is quite good. However, each ad brings inquiries in addition to immediate sales, and inquiries provide names for a direct mail list. Fran and Betty keep a cross-reference file on each item advertised, the name of the purchaser, the names of inquirers and their possible future needs. If you get six calls on one item — which is common — and you keep a record, the next time you buy a similar piece you don't have to advertise at all.

4. Service and good will are at the heart of sound mail order dealings. You must ship promptly and safely. Betty and Fran find that United Parcel Service works best for them. Other dealers have found Greyhound and Trailways very reliable. Few, except those who can send lightweight paper goods via first class, even consider the U.S. mails. Bubble pack and padded materials are an important investment, too. Good service includes courteous refunds, Christmas notes to customers, and an overall atmosphere of friendliness.

5. As for copy, make it readable and try not to repeat merchandise. If something doesn't sell, don't repeat it, at least not immediately.

This is the same principle that motivates shop dealers to put aside certain items into inventory.

6. A rare item, not immediately identifiable by copy, is best described with a photo. Some merchandise has to be seen to be sold, and for this it is a good idea to do at least some shows. A built-up advertising image will provide a certain recognition to one's booth, giving the mail order dealer at a show a minor celebrity status.

The Catalogue as a Mail Order Medium

A number of specialties lend themselves especially well to being sold through catalogues. The catalogues can be as uncomplicated as offset or mimeographed lists, with or without lengthy annotations, or the glossy booklets that become collectibles in their own right. Book and manuscript dealers are among the most frequent users of the list and catalogue system; for example, Alton Ketchum of Cos Cob, Connecticut, and his daughter Deborah Lambert, of MacLean, Virginia.

Mr. Ketchum, a former advertising executive and lifelong history buff, in recent years has devoted his energies to enlarging his own vast collection of historic manuscripts while selling manuscripts through a lovingly annotated catalogue, issued several times a year. Although Deborah Lambert, née Ketchum, grew up in a history-filled home, it was not until about three years ago that her father's enthusiasm and her immediate need for an income-producing activity spurred her to launch her own mail order dealership. A donation of stock from Connecticut helped to fill the first catalogue, but since then father and daughter have run completely separate businesses, each taking a somewhat different approach.

Debbie Lambert focuses on Civil War newspapers, maps, and prints, and likes to issue frequent short catalogues with very brief annotations. She finds advertising in general publications a waste of time, and so limits herself to *The Antiques Trader Weekly* and *The Civil War Times,* considering the latter her best medium because it always brings "a bundle of replies."

Alton Ketchum's catalogues are longer and more strongly personalized productions, issued at less frequent intervals. "I tend to discourse a lot about historical background matters, and while I stick to a simple offset job, I do make a fetish of sending everything — catalogues, orders — by first-class. I feel this conveys a certain impression of quality and leadership." In addition to Debbie's advertising media, he uses the bookseller's bible, *The AB Bookman's Yearbook*, and the magazine *Early American Life*. His catalogue brings much special-order business, and the research involved in this feeds his allied career as a writer of historical articles.

Most manuscript buying by dealers, according to Alton Ketchum, is done through auctions, though he advises novices that there are great caches of less scarce but nonetheless interesting historical papers to be obtained from libraries, town halls, county building basements, university collections that are about to be microfilmed, and private acquisitions dispersed to settle estates. "One technique for the impecunious buyer is to find out where files are being microfilmed and to offer to take them at low cost or for free before they are destroyed." According to Mr. Ketchum, a young man he met some years ago boasted of a haul from Columbia University worth $100,000. He adds, "And I know for certain that a man in Virginia saved fourteen bound volumes of the New York *Herald*, eighteen forty-eight to fifty-seven, from being burned — because I paid him four hundred dollars for them!"

For those wondering if a newcomer, without benefit of a lifetime of experience or a paternal helping hand, can actually earn a good living from mail order catalogue selling, there is the sweet smell of success permeating the sunny apartment, overlooking New York's Central Park, where Allen and Hilary Weiner conduct their mail order business.

Back in 1970, both Allen and Hilary were still employed as less-than-enthusiastic public school teachers. Cameras held no special meaning for either of them until Allen bought a Nikon to do some hobby photography and began to subscribe to *Popular Photography*. In its pages he saw an ad for an antique camera auction at Sotheby's PB Eighty-Four gallery. "I was ripe for collecting *something*," exclaimed Allen, who sometimes seems about to explode with pleasure over his mode of living and working. His memory of the Bantam Special bought for $110 at that first auction is sweetened by the recently recorded auction price of $36,000 for a similar model!

Shortly after that auction, Hilary picked up a camera for $5.00 in a neighborhood shop as a Valentine's Day present for Allen. This set off a period of intense and perspicacious collecting. For example, Allen quickly learned to talk to people at house sales and flea markets, to find out about things beyond what was on display. It was such a conversation with an exhibitor at the famous Brimfield Flea Market, in Massachusetts, that led the Weiners to their first big coup— an entire photographer's studio of cameras and equipment!

The Weiners' instinct for quality, trends, buying, and selling became ever more sharply honed. In 1972, they decided to issue a catalogue as an experimental venture, as much to sell off duplicate merchandise as to see if they could really consider their avocation a potential full-time vocation. Allen was still teaching, and that first four-page brochure listing thirty-one items was cranked out on the school mimeo machine and mailed to a list of 100 possible buyers, bought from the National Directory of Camera Collectors. (Note: Many magazines, clubs, and list brokers rent or sell special-interest lists.) To the Weiners' delight, one collector bought almost the entire catalogue lot, about a thousand dollars' worth. No small profit for one employed and one unemployed schoolteacher!

Since 1972, the Weiners' catalogue has grown into a handsomely illustrated booklet issued four times a year and mailed to 350 people, each of whom pays $4.00 per copy. The price helps defray expenses for photos, printing, and mailing and also discourages idle curiosity seekers. Gross sales from each quarterly issue have climbed to a very respectable five-digit figure, with customers usually calling in their orders within two weeks of the catalogue's issuance. Since customers pay not only for the catalogue but for shipping, this is an almost no-expense operation. The catalogue, ads in antiques papers (more to buy than to sell), active membership in the New York Photographic Historical Society and the National Stereo Association, all bring lots of business.

Many things don't stay around long enough ever to get into the catalogue. Contacts reach around the world, and both Allen and Hilary consider their extensive buying and selling trips a pleasurable aspect of their business. Though many photographica dealers can be seen at general antiques shows, these have little place in the Weiners' scheme of things. Occasionally, they rent a booth at a particularly interesting show, mainly to be there during set-up time and thus be able to buy. This points up a problem inherent in their long-range planning. An increasing tightening-up of sources has already forced the Weiners to include some twentieth-century cameras in their catalogues, and they are keeping a sharp eye out for related merchandise, such as scientific equipment, just in case the photographic profit bubble bursts.

The Catalogue on a Grand Scale

Most mail order cataloguers, as already indicated, start out with relatively small list-type mailings. Not so Peter Rakelbusch, of Hadley, Massachusetts, whose vision of his future as an art deco dealer includes such sophisticated concepts as a computerized customer file system and worldwide connections. Peter's very first catalogue, published in 1977, was a splendidly clever, profusely illustrated showcase for some 500 pieces of art deco ware, assiduously "picked" at flea markets, house sales, and shows all over the country. Whether $1 or $500, all items were lovingly photographed and meticulously and wittily described. Buyers of that first limited edition of 1000 ($2.50 a copy) recognized its value as an unusual, highly collectible price guide. Here are some of the ingredients that added up to a respectable sale for the catalogue itself and for its contents:

1. A catchy title that left plenty of room for expansion: 21st Century Antiques.

2. Stylish and refreshingly humorous writing and very attractive graphics.

3. A well thought-out press campaign, with releases that read like stories and didn't merely make a pitch for the business. This resulted in national coverage, not only in antiques magazines and newspapers but in such magazines as *House and Garden* and *Gentleman's Quarterly*.

Since Peter is very personable and speaks as well as he writes, press coverage also led to a number of television interviews. The results from the first catalogue were sufficiently encouraging for him immediately to set a second one in motion.

Lest anyone hasten into planning a catalogue that costs $2500 to put together (without inventory costs), it would be best to keep in mind that Peter Rakelbusch did not embark on his venture without previous training and experience. His business and management skills had been developed during a stint he served as a bank book-keeper. His knowledge of antiques and the antiques trade came by way of a two-year apprenticeship as a runner at the Amherst Auction Galleries. What's more, good publicity and sales notwithstanding, 21st Century Antiques has not moved forward without setbacks. Neither the first nor the second catalogue (expanded to 2500 copies) was a complete sellout, so Peter has had to take both catalogues and merchandise to occasional shows, where people can see for themselves. The rising interest in art deco and art nouveau has also caused the usual problem of stock replacement; to offset this, Peter has started several Mini-Logs. One of these is devoted strictly to books on art deco, which means that each listing can result in many sales, not just one. He is also considering a catalogue of fine contemporary crafts, because this fits beneath his company title and would again eliminate the problem of replacement.

Peter Rakelbusch steps out of the pages of his catalogue, to meet the public at a large show. The sale of catalogues alone defrays his expenses.

A Catalogue Checklist

Before we leave the subject of mail order catalogues, here are a few summing-up words of wisdom for future cataloguers:

1. Group your items carefully. Throw in at least a few real bargains!

2. Spend a lot of care on your cover and your introductory copy, for this is where you build your image for this and future efforts.

3. Photos are an invaluable selling aid. However, you don't need to go to the expense of color, if your black-and-white pictures are clear and well focused. (See Photography Know-How, in Part II, Resources.)

4. Be sure your catalogue includes a well-designed, crystal-clear order card.

5. Count all your costs before you have your catalogue printed. For example, make up a dummy of the exact paper, number of pages, inserts, and so on, and take the dummy to the post office. You may find that by using a lighter weight paper or reducing the contents by

All types of antiques and collectibles can be sold through catalogues. For details about the mail order auction catalogue at left, see Chapter 5.

a page or two, you can save a bundle of money on postage.

6. Don't depend on yourself as the one and only proofreader. You'll be too tired to recognize all mistakes. Enlist friends and colleagues to preview and also proofread for printing and price errors.

A well-designed, crystal-clear response card is a must for a good catalogue. A touch of cleverness and humor won't hurt.

CHAPTER 4

❖ ❖ ❖

Everybody's
an Appraiser
But . . .

Appraising is as wide as the range of human interest and as
wide as man's proclivity for placing value on objects.
— Dexter MacBride, Executive Vice President,
American Society of Appraisers

Everyone who buys — collector, dealer, tag or house sale coordinator, auctioneer — fills the fundamental role of an appraiser: evaluating objects on the basis of knowledge of quality, authenticity, style,
provenance, and price trends. Without this knowledge, you cannot
buy well or consign well. What, then, separates those who appraise
to buy and sell from the professional appraiser?

The professional evaluates property with a specific purpose in
mind — replacement in case of theft, fire, or damage; disposal for
personal or circumstantial reasons; archival value. Furthermore, the
professional appraiser documents the evaluation with written and
illustrative materials and in a manner and form acceptable to lawyers
and insurance officials.

The profession as a whole embraces people who deal in real estate,
industrial property, anything and everything that is likely to be lost,

stolen, destroyed, disposed of, or depreciated. It is only the growing awareness, during the last decade, of the investment value of antiques and other objets d'art and the tightening of insurance regulations in regard to personal property valuation that have lifted appraisal out of the almost exclusive realm of real estate.

Does this mean a solid career opportunity exists for the appraiser specializing in the area of antiques and related personal property items? Since appraising is part of the decision-making process for dealers, auctioneers, and house sales specialists, can they, once they are versed in the methodology of preparing reports, enjoy dual careers?

Because of the growing number of people relying on fee appraisals for their full-time incomes, the answer to the first question is obviously yes.

However, the answer to the second question is also yes, if only because many who have other interests do, in fact, also appraise. Those with a professional attitude toward the entire antiques-collectibles business recognize the inherent conflict of interest that exists when a dealer is called in to appraise a collection he may want to buy, and the consequent necessity to apply the strictest sort of self-censorship when functions threaten to overlap. In short, any activity beyond the purpose of the requested appraisal must be kept separate and apart. The American Society of Appraisers stipulates in its guidelines for members that appraisal reports must include a "statement of the appraiser's disinterestedness in the property appraised." If the appraiser does have an interest, present or future, the society says he must so inform the potential client before accepting an assignment.

THE QUALITIES AN APPRAISER SHOULD POSSESS

The following prerequisites were most often cited by working appraisers. The order is random, not ranked.

1. New York appraiser Timothy Tetlow talks of developing an "awakened eye." Isabella Charbenau Warren of Seattle, Washington, refers to a need for a "private eye for taste." Call it what you will,

one of the appraiser's prime qualifications for making judgments is a sense for the quality of an object. This is not so much inherent as it is cultivated through environmental and educational influences.

2. Tact will go a long way in handling a situation where something offered for appraisal has more sentimental than monetary value. As Mrs. Warren states in an educational tape made for the American Society of Appraisers, "You have to be almost a psychiatrist." The appraiser who knows that the vase the client has inherited from Aunt Milly is worthless or of an inferior period must learn to temper truth with tact. Surely there is *something* positive you can say, such as, "I can see why you love it but I'm afraid that tiny knick detracts from its financial value," or, if it's really old and beat-up–looking, "I hesitate to recommend that you invest in the sort of restoration required for top dollar sale."

3. A bent for scholarship probably understates the prodigious amount of information a good appraiser must continuously absorb and digest. The first-mentioned sense for the quality of an object, no matter how thoroughly developed through courses and work experience, must nevertheless be augmented with constant research. The appraiser with even the most extensive personal library will have to make more than occasional trips to other reference sources.

4. Analytical ability is needed to translate one's knowledge and observation into an appraisal that provides the desired information. Identification and provenance of an item, its price history as judged from auction records, and its condition — all these must be weighed on the value scale and the final figure adjusted according to the purpose of the appraisal (usually on the high side for insurance, the low wide for estates).

5. Every profession has its terminology, and the appraiser must be conversant with these value criteria:

Replacement value: The cost of replacing what you own in the present marketplace.

Fair market value: The price that a buyer will pay. This can vary enormously according to the location of the property, the probable marketplace, or the most favorable possible marketplace.

Liquidation or *Distress value:* The price likely to be realized at an immediate or forced sale, such as an auction.

Subjective value: The emotional worth of an item to its owner.

Archival value: Most commonly associated with private and institutional collections, this is based on the qualities that make something worth owning.

There are other terms less specific to the antiques business; for example, depreciation costs, reproduction costs, cash or book value.

6. Personal integrity, as Oklahoma City appraiser Juanita Brown puts it in an ASA Valutape, revolves around character, and "character determines what you would be if there were no such thing as retribution." The separation, discussed above, of the appraiser's buying interests from the appraisal report is vital to the maintenance of a reputation for personal and professional integrity. The matter of referral fees for recommending appraisal collections and estates to particular auction houses is another touchy area.

Integrity is also involved in the way an appraisal is made. No reputable appraiser, for example, will evaluate anything not personally seen, or make on-the-spot judgments about things requiring in-depth research; nor will he evaluate an object outside his personal field of expertise without enlisting a qualified colleague.

7. Although literary skill is unnecessary, detail and exactness in the written appraisal are important. Items should be described as specifically as possible, with attention paid to number, maker, period, style, size, special marks, and other characteristics. With a general dictionary and several reference books on fine and decorative arts at hand, the appraiser can reach the right balance between simplicity and authoritativeness.

8. It takes clients to build a business, so the ability and willingness to make and follow up on contacts in a dignified manner cannot be underestimated in projecting potential success. Calling on lawyers, bankers, insurance agents, moving company executives, is all part of getting established. Good contacts can be made through civic, recreational, and business organizations, by writing articles for insurance trade journals, or giving talks to adult education groups. It's a good policy to call on people in the business community, but private individuals are likely to regard with suspicion contacts smacking of solicitation.

Good will, leading to referrals, can be created if you offer clients a bit more than they paid for — a book or booklet about the type of collection appraised, follow-ups in the form of reviews of new books, announcements of interesting events, and so on, sent as a way of keeping in touch. Often appraisers, either individually or as a group, donate their services for appraisals at shows or charity parties.

HOW AN APPRAISER ACQUIRES QUALIFICATIONS AND SKILLS

Since collectors, dealers, and auctioneers must learn to appraise objects if they are to function well, any one of these roles is excellent basic training for an appraiser. If this practical experience is coupled

This sketch by artist Stokely Webster was Harold Jaffee's only "payment" for donating his services at an appraisal party for the Huntington Township Art League. Photographed with Mr. Jaffee's permission

with courses in art and antiques and background reading, you may well find that you can walk into a house and make a reasonably accurate assessment of what it contains and what those contents are likely to be worth.

So far, so good. But how do you establish your credibility so that someone will actually ask you to make the appraisal?

If you have a shop or sell at local shows, you can put up a sign that says I Do APPRAISALS, since there are neither state nor federal government regulations against doing this. However, though you may know how to identify objects, nothing has prepared you for the mechanics of doing the appraisal. How do you learn the fine points of the different types of appraisals? What is the accepted format? What if the insurance company won't accept your appraisal, or one you have done comes under question in a court case? These are some of the questions that frighten many a would-be appraiser.

Happily, help is at hand.

To start with, your friendly Internal Revenue Service has two free publications: #561, *Valuation of Donated Property;* and *A Procedure to Be Used as a Guideline by All Appraisers of Donated Property.* Also, and without even leaving your home, you can avail yourself of some excellent material compiled by the American Society of Appraisers (P. O. Box 17265, Washington, D.C. 20041). While you can't become a member of this organization or the other major appraisal organization, the Appraisers Association of America, until you've put in several years as a nonmember appraiser, the ASA educational materials are available to any individual or group. Monograph #7, *Commentary on Personal Property Appraisal,* for example, offers a wealth of information, including sample appraisals, for only $2.50.

My suggestion is to send for the above-mentioned monograph right away, along with the ASA's list of other publications and cassettes.

The Appraisers Association of America (AAA) does not publish educational materials. However, if you live near New York try to be on hand for one of its monthly meetings, held in the evening. (Call the office, at 541 Lexington Avenue, to get the dates.) A serious newcomer would not be turned away from attending at least one meeting.

JuanitA C. Brown   Appraiser

Route 4, Box 532, Oklahoma City, Okla., 73111, **405/424-3795**

June 15, 1974

Mr. John P. Thomas
589935 Quail Creek Road
Oklahoma City, Oklahoma 73121

Dear Mr. Thomas:

Please find enclosed Appraisal Report of the Eighteenth Century Secretary for your Insurance Schedule.

This Appraisal Report does not concern itself in any way or manner with the known title or ownership of the appraised article.

Please advise if I may be of further service.

Sincerely,

Juanita C. Brown

JCB:s

A covering letter expressing the appraiser's personal disinterest is standard procedure. Reprinted from Monograph #7, courtesy of the American Society of Appraisers

Authorized Appraisal

This Is To Certify That I,

JuAnita C. Brown, Appraiser,

have carefully examined all articles and personal property listed and in my judgment, without any personal interest, declare the current value of each item at the request of

name ___John Paul and Mary Lee Thomas___

address ___589935 Quail Creek Road___
___Oklahoma City, Oklahoma 73121___

ARTICLE	DESCRIPTION	APPRAISED VALUE
1	ENGLISH BLACK LACQUER SECRETARY Circa 1750 Height 7 Feet 10 Inches Width 3 Feet 3 Inches Depth 1 Foot 10 Inches	
	Exotic fowl, flowering branches and landscapes in gilt and red Chinoiserie decoration, cabinet interior pale rust. The upper case section has a broken pediment, centered and flanked with urn finials. Original glazed doors of arched design conceals a group of pigeon-holes, candle slides, nests of drawers and filing compartments, over a sloping fall-front opening to disclose a flat writing surface, a well, pigeon-holes and drawers. Two short and two long drawers form lower case, with pierced escutcheons and bail brasses, mounted on bracket feet.	
	Condition: Exceptional, with minor chips and leg repairs	
	Provenance: Purchased in 1935 from private owner in London, England, by Mrs. Ernest Fain. Sold at auction in 1969 to a Oklahoma City private collector.	$ 15,000.00

Note: *Appraisal made for Insurance Replacement Value*

JuAnita C. Brown 🌓 Appraiser

4401 N.E. 36th St., Route 4, Box 532, Oklahoma City, Okla., 73111 (405) 424-3795

MEMBER:
Appraisers Association of
America/American Society of
Appraisers/National Association
of Dealers in Antiques, Inc.
The Valuers Consortium

SIGNED ___Juanita C. Brown___

DATE ___June 15,___ 19_74_

Here is Appraiser Brown's evaluation of the appearance, condition, provenance, and replacement value of a single piece of furniture. Reprinted from Monograph #7, courtesy of the American Society of Appraisers

L. M. Hotchkiss & Associates

Appraisers

L. M. HOTCHKISS
FASA
FSVA

681 MARKET STREET
SAN FRANCISCO, CALIF. 94105
Telephone (415) 362-6979

March 1, 1974

Mr. and Mrs. A.B.C. Smith
1000 Carmel Rd.
Pebble Beach, California

Dear Mr. and Mrs. Smith:

In accordance with our agreement, we have made an insurance appraisal of the contents of your residence at the above address, furs and jewelry excepted, as of

January 15, 1974

The totals, taxes included, are:

Art Objects:		X Dollars
Art Objects (Breakable):		X Dollars
Unscheduled Items		
Replacement Cost:	X Dollars	
Insurable Value:		X Dollars
Total Insurable Value:		X Dollars

The values set forth represent the best information obtainable as to prevailing costs in this region.

The photographs are for ready reference in the event of a claim under any insurance policy.

The appraiser has no financial interest in the items appraised and does not contemplate any such interest in the future.

Respectfully submitted,

L. M. HOTCHKISS & ASSOCIATES

By_____ FASA

...nce Broker

This letter sums up the categories of objects appraised by L. M. Hotchkiss & Associates. Both this and previously illustrated appraisal include photographs. Reprinted from Monograph #7, courtesy of the American Society of Appraisers

A.B.C. Smith - 1973   2

ART OBJECTS, CONT'D.

Dining Room

Photo #40

1   Custom, carved walnut dining suite
     with fruit and floral motif:

          Oval extension table 84" long   )
          with 4 - 16" skirted leaves   )
)
          Buffet with 3 center drawers   )
          and side cabinets; 84" wide   )
)
          Side server with single drawer;)
          60" wide   )
)
          Two host and ten side chairs   ) $ 9,500

Photo 43

1   Pair Sheffield 11" oval entree dishes,
     gadroon trim - by Matthew Boulton   -
     (signed). Circa 1800.
     Condition very good.   800

Photo 44

1   Pair 27½", two-branch, three-socket
     candlesticks to match above.
     Condition very good.   1,250

Throughout - Art Objects

Books:

1   Holinshed's Chronicles - 1577.
     Vols. I & II.
     Known as the "Shakespeare Edition".
     Tooled leather. Condition good.   1,500

L. M. HOTCHKISS & ASSOCIATES — APPRAISERS

An appraisal of the contents of an entire household requires describing objects a room at a time. This one took up a number of pages; some appraisals are actually catalogues. Reprinted from Monograph #7, courtesy of the American Society of Appraisers

What about formal education?

Some college art departments, aware of the need to guide students into areas with employment opportunities, have introduced appraisal studies as part of the art history program. Hofstra University, on Long Island, New York, is a case in point.

Large auction houses, like Sotheby Parke Bernet and Christie, Manson and Woods, have developed overseas courses that emphasize the handling of objects along with more academic studies. Similar courses have begun to find their way into less expensive and more accessible situations on this side of the Atlantic. Most of these remain within the college extension or adult education domain; since

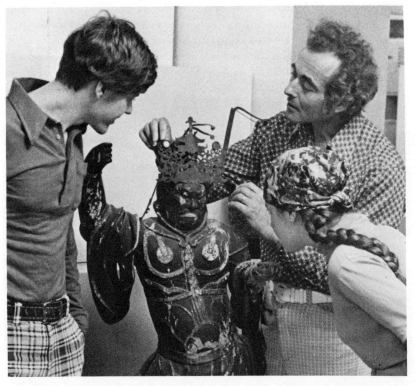

The Hofstra University Art Exchange reaches into the community's living rooms and attics to provide students with real appraising experience. Evaluations are made as a joint effort. Photograph, Murray Duitz

these are geared directly to student needs and requests, it depends very much on the student to voice and elucidate his needs.

For a practical self-study approach, nothing really beats attending auction previews, practicing writing down descriptions of objects and then comparing them with the professional cataloguer's work. Where has the professional been more specific, more authoritative? If you can't make estimates, do you know where to do research?

INVESTMENT AND OVERHEAD FOR APPRAISERS

According to Harold Jaffee, coordinator of the Appraisal Studies and Interior Design Certificate Program at Long Island University's C. W. Post Center in Greenville, Long Island, an appraiser's basic

Appraiser Sigmund Rothschild does research and sees clients in an impressive, high-ceilinged New York City duplex.

tool kit can be put together for about $100. This would include a black or fluorescent light to scan out repairs, a magnifier or loupe, an x ray apparatus, a scale to weigh up to 100 ounces of silver, a knife, and lots and lots of pencils.

The appraiser's biggest and continual investment, like that of anyone in the field of art-antiques-collectibles, is in building up a library of books and auction catalogues, subscribing to a variety of publications, and attending seminars.

Since it is important to convey to clients a sense of professionalism and integrity and high quality, your stationery, though not a major investment, should be well designed. The image created by your stationery will be strongly reinforced by the physical appearance of the information. For anyone who can afford it, an IBM Selectric typewriter with several different elements will do wonders to give your appraisals the look of having been printed.

A tool not to be overlooked is a camera. A visual inventory to accompany an appraisal is valuable and indeed necessary. (See Photography Know-How in Part II, Resources.)

Finally, there is the matter of the place from which you conduct your business. An impressive, well-located setting, like appraiser Sigmund Rothschild's rather baronial Central Park West duplex, won't hurt, but it is by no means necessary. For the most part, you will go where the client is rather than the other way around, so in the long run it is you, your bearing, and your knowledge that will have to carry the day.

THE FRANCHISE APPROACH TO APPRAISAL

For those who like things all wrapped up in a neat package — and as an indication of the obvious career potential of the appraisal field — a group known as the Heritage Antique and Appraisal Society (6151 Wilson Mills Road, Cleveland, Ohio 44143) has put together a rather interesting package that trains people to become franchised directors who operate under the society's aegis in the areas of both appraisals and estate liquidations. The franchise costs $5500, which entitles the future director to participate in a lecture-training program, receive a packet of printed reference materials, and use the society's imprint on stationery and appraisal forms. There is also some on-site supervision. In addition to the initial investment, there is a percentage of earnings that society members are asked to kick back into an educational fund.

The decision about the worth of such an investment is, of necessity, a very personal one. The directorships are still too limited at present for any serious assessment. Probably the society's good and bad aspects are best summed up by its first franchised director, Harry T. Coffield, of Worthington, Ohio. Mr. Coffield signed up for the franchise because he thought its concept an excellent one. He did not feel put upon at having to draw on his own resources to implement it. As he explained in a long letter, "It became apparent to me . . . that the programs outlined; i.e., lecture scripts, slides, reference materials, were not complete and that those that were complete required some additional work on my part to bring them to a level of sophistication I felt necessary. This did not seem unreasonable in that the basic concept was there and I enjoyed the research and preparation involved."

Mr. Coffield went on to say that "the society has had slower progress than forecast in the selling of directorships because (1) the elements of the program were underdeveloped at the point where marketing began. Further research, professional editing and field testing, coupled with expanded publicity, would have made the initial marketing effort more fruitful. (2) Too many of the directors and potential directors are seeking an easy road to success; desiring a ready-made program which requires little work. This is not to be, and would not be the case even if the concept were further developed as outlined above."

In addition to his willingness to bring his own creativity and initiative to the franchise. Mr. Coffield has the kind of background and experience to which the society's founders had hoped to appeal. He has a long-standing interest in antiques, is well educated, with many years of invaluable experience in sales and in public speaking. Moreover, he was able and willing almost to double the franchise investment, "coast" for a year, and, once set up as a full-time director (he started on a part-time basis), work ten to twelve hours a day, six days a week, fifty weeks a year. So far, not enough people with Mr. Coffield's abilities and potential have been persuaded that the support of the Heritage setup makes it more attractive than the totally independent route.

APPRAISING AS A FULL-TIME, PART-TIME, DUAL CAREER

Three Profiles

I've lost count of the number of young people I've encountered who equated an exciting career in antiques with working for a large auction house in New York, preferably Sotheby Parke Bernet. Timothy Tetlow, who used to work for the venerated auction house, is living proof that, as coveted and hard to get as such jobs are, not everyone who gets there remains in this antiques equivalent of the Promised Land.

Having started at the bottom of the Sotheby ladder — numbering, handling, wrapping objects, and listing them in preparation for handling at the Madison Avenue branch; moving over to the then-new PB Eighty-Four branch and becoming familiar with decorative arts and collectible objects; organizing one of the company's first large house sales — all this invaluable practical experience and its attendant connections have helped to put the Timothy Tetlow Appraisal Company on a solid, full-time, self-supporting footing.

Just as a job at Sotheby Parke Bernet does not ensure enduring career satisfaction to everyone, neither does it eliminate the risks and hard work and discouragement for those striking out on their own. "I went down to Wall Street and personally visited custom departments of banks to get on their lists, and at first it's rather discouraging," Tim Tetlow recalled. "At first you just sit by that telephone until it starts to ring. For me, the needed boost came through a note about a stein collection someone wanted appraised. It sounded like the usual run of bar steins, and someone else had in fact turned it down. It turned out to be a collection of old seventeenth- and eighteenth-century ivory, faience-mounted tankards — some one hundred and fifty to two hundred pieces, all worth from five hundred to eleven thousand dollars each, to be identified and catalogued. I had some catalogues from a similar Sotheby Parke Bernet sale as reference guidelines, and the owner was very pleased with my appraisal."

Timothy regards actual work experience, such as he had, better than the more academic training. He feels a busy antique shop would be a good apprenticeship also. "The main thing is learning about the dynamics of the market. This world is a mixture of art and business, and I don't see enough emphasis on business around. I've always been very business-oriented, but I also love fine things and I feel the two can and do mix."

Since the Tetlow letterhead also mentions consultation and brokerage, I asked how this worked into his scheme of things. "I will, under selected circumstances, broker a piece of art which needs special handling," he told me. "I do this as a separate part of the appraisal business, on a standard ten percent commission. I feel very strongly about avoiding any sort of commingling [mixing of functions], and, as an active member of the Appraisers Association of America, I am very concerned with improving standards of qualification and conduct." He does not, however, believe in licensing; just thorough self-policing.

When Timothy Tetlow does an appraisal that includes ancient coins, he calls on another Sotheby Parke Bernet "dropout," Beth Weingast. After a six-year career in the coin and metal and miniature painting department at Sotheby's, she became a psychiatric social worker, while maintaining her interest in antiquities and coins through private, part-time appraisal work. Her career switch wasn't made on a snap decision, for she enjoyed the nature of her auction work and the prestige. The fairly low salary scale bothered her somewhat but not as much as the object orientation. "I come from a middle-class intellectual family, and the elitism and the fact that people were subservient to objects was very disturbing to me." And so Beth, whose original degree from Boston University was in archeology — "that was the right degree at the time, since Sotheby's was starting an ancient coin department and was willing to send me to England for a year's training" — went to school again, this time for a master's in social work. She is currently a social work representative with a foster care agency located just thirty blocks from her former stamping grounds.

Beth admits that most people thought she was crazy to leave Sotheby's for the back-to-school routine, but it has worked out very well for her. "I've been lucky in juggling two careers and probably enjoy both because I have an opportunity to see different spectrums of behavior and interaction. If there is any similarity between social work and art, it is that in both you are willing to probe and to dig. You take nothing on a superficial level, and in that sense art, though less scientific, does train you to be careful and to research."

Even with a full-time career, she says she is able to do several appraising jobs a month. Because many people in her social work milieu are involved in art and antiques, her new career has actually opened up a whole new area of clientele.

Beth's appraisals range from ancient to modern American coins, and her fees vary, hinging on a combination of the time and value involved. Appraisal demands run from simple piece-by-piece evaluation to full catalogues. Beth Weingast's private life is also a fusion of the different parts of her world. She met her husband, a psychiatrist, through her second career, though it is their mutual interest in art (he's a dedicated rug collector) that brought them together.

Timothy Tetlow and Beth Weingast are the sort of well-informed, ethics-conscious young blood that Mrs. Regina Hayes welcomes to membership in the Appraisers Association of America, of which she is past president. Mrs. Hayes, a sprightly, very warm woman, seems to enjoy the many facets that make up her own life — appraiser, auctioneer, mother, and grandmother. Originally, she and her husband studied to be chiropractors, but the practice of this profession was obstructed by many roadblocks at the time. Mr. Hayes decided to follow up on his childhood experience of attending auctions with his father by becoming an auctioneer. Mrs. Hayes, in the meantime, pursued a growing interest in antiques.

At first she collected for herself, always reading up on things. "I would go with my husband to check out the antique items for an auction, and when I began doing appraisals, he accompanied me to those." After her husband died, she took up the auctioneer's gavel, and today she is a free-lance auctioneer and appraiser. The auctions are not limited to antiques, but her appraisals are all in the personal property and antiques area. She cites the importance of reading up on *all* levels of collecting even if you specialize in very fine antiques. Not long ago, she saw in someone's sewing box a little tape measure with a picture on it. Because she keeps up with the whole field of collecting interests, she was able to recognize its value as a memorabilia item.

She also finds that being ethical brings its own rewards. "I love

Appraiser Timothy Tetlow believes that actually handling an object is essential to sound evaluation. Without closer inspection, one can't be sure: Is it an eighteenth- or a nineteenth-century Windsor chair?

finding something of good value and showing people what they have." She illustrated this with the story of the Chinese bowl recently found in a widow's home. "I told her, 'I wouldn't give you fifty dollars for that, and when she asked, 'Why?' I told her, 'Because I would be *stealing* it.' "

In addition to being active in the AAA, Mrs. Hayes is a member of the ASA, as well as the National Auctioneers Society. Her family might well be dubbed an all-antiques one: all three of her daughters have in one way or another followed in their mother and father's footsteps. Daughter Beverly studied fine arts but shelved career plans for marriage. While her husband was studying for his Ph.D., she decided to open an antique shop in an old tea room, but first she organized a co-op nursery for her two children, so that she could devote full time to the business. When the family moved to Michigan, she became a show dealer and formed an antiques dealers group. Like Beth Weingast, she recently went back to school to study psychiatric social work, though she continues to keep her hand in antiques. Another daughter, Iris Marness, became a jewelry dealer, and the youngest Hayes daughter, Helene, free-lances as Mrs. Hayes' auction bookkeeper.

CHAPTER 5

❖ ❖ ❖

The Impresarios: Auctioneers, House Sale Organizers, Show Promoters

Throughout history, the method of bringing a maximum number of people together to bid competitively on merchandise offered up one piece at a time has proved an efficient and convenient method for realizing the highest possible profit. As we have seen, the auction experience is excellent preparation for the fulfillment of a variety of antiques-related ambitions. For many more, it is a means in itself.

The glamour associated with the auction sales in New York, London, Geneva, and Paris has been reflected in Los Angeles and San Francisco, Dallas, and such Midwestern cities as Detroit, Milwaukee, and Chicago. In spite of this, the Manhattan scene is the one beckoning most charismatically, with 400 applicants likely to clamor after even the humblest openings. Those who make it aboard with the corporate auction house don't always become auctioneers.

Timothy Tetlow, whom we met in the last chapter, considers it great luck that he came to Sotheby Parke Bernet just as that company was developing its lower-priced branch. "If I had not been sent to PB Eighty-Four to work under its first director, John Stair, I might have remained a cataloguer for years instead of getting a feel for the

Of the 400 job openings at Sotheby Parke Bernet, that of attending one of the reception desks, to which prospective clients bring things for inspection, is a much sought-after one.

The main salesroom at Sotheby Parke Bernet bears all the earmarks of a large theater, with chief auctioneer John Marion regally enthroned. Objets d'art likely to fall under the hammer range from antiquities to furniture, from Old Master paintings to those from a more contemporary school.

whole picture — bringing in business, following the object into the house, onto the block, and until it went out again."

It is this familiarity with the object and the market that Tim Tetlow regards as the essence of auctioneering, much more than the mechanics: "That's simply a matter of timing, developing your own style. The main thing is that you've got to know what you're selling. If you don't know the value of an object, you might spend three minutes trying to get two thousand dollars for an item worth only two hundred. When you're selling for a volume operation where you deal with five hundred lots a day, with perhaps twenty or more items to the lot, you've pretty much got to have everything synchronized."

This sort of large-corporation organizational experience, besides being generally unavailable, is also unappealing to many. The auction business they envision may include a good many run-of-the-mill sales — and so do the glamour auctions, for that matter — but the overhead will be a lot lower and the pressures considerably less. What's more, a number of outstandingly successful people did start out in hired halls and barns, and they serve as inspiration for newcomers who like to visualize their futures on a grand scale. Sometimes a single break in getting a particularly fine and much sought-after collection will put a country auctioneer into the national limelight. Other estate offers follow, buyers come from farther afield, in turn bringing still more and better estates, and on and on. The Robert Skinner Auction Barn in Bolton, Massachusetts, is a notable example.

HOW INDEPENDENT AUCTIONEERS GET STARTED

Without pun intended, the most common way to learn the auction business is in the school of hard knocks. You go to a lot of auctions and observe, get an inside view by buying and consigning, and work into some kind of helping job. Many of the auctioneering schools and courses address themselves more to those who will be selling off livestock instead of antiques, though there are workshops conducted by auctioneers particularly active in antiques. Auctioneers graduating from such programs look on them as a sort of graduate degree to cap off the school-of-hard-knocks experiences.

Even more important than whether to seek out a formalized course is the decision about whether to be a roving auctioneer — one who hires space or goes where the property is for sale — or to set up a regular auction room, with a set schedule of sales. Let's look first at some roving auctioneers.

THE ROVING AUCTIONEER

Classique Auctions is an outgrowth of Sheila Goldman and Carol and Don Saltzman's Classique Car Exchange, a dealership in antique cars and related collectibles that dates back to 1971. Initially, it was the women who together bought a Model T Ford, as an investment against inflation. This was followed by other purchases, and within a year Don retired from twenty-five years in the broadcasting and motion picture business and the three friends and neighbors became incorporated partners in the Classic Car Exchange.

Working out of their home base in Hewlett, Long Island, they formed national contacts through membership in various automobile collector clubs (a check on this category in *The Encyclopedia of Associations* will be an eye-opener) and by participating in automotive flea markets. They also consigned cars to automotive auctions.

"Within a year we learned all the ins and outs of the car auction business," Don explained. "While we saw rings and knockdowns [see Glossary] and a lot of other so-called tricks, those auctions did supply a marketplace in an otherwise very tough-to-crack market."

Eventually Don and Sheila began to run a few car auctions themselves, as part of their business. They say there is a tremendous amount of money to be made here, but they also cite the capital risks for fairgrounds and ballroom rentals, security and other payroll items, and advertising.

In these bigger and bigger auctions, they also saw the profit source shifting from commissions to the "gate." On one auction they spent some $35,000 to attract 20,000 people, whose $2.00 admission was the real profit. The massive production quality of these auctions was also reflected in the rest of the antique car business, and Don and

Sheila and Carol felt themselves squeezed by the big operators. They wanted to maintain their contact with the collector and they did want to become active auctioneers, but in a less grandiose style.

To reach a broader collector-hobbyist market, they had to expand their automobile background. When they heard that the International Auction Institute was running an intensive summer auction session in conjunction with the University of Massachusetts, with emphasis on antiques, Don and Sheila enrolled. It was just what they needed: "We studied from eight in the morning until midnight, and everyone was very giving. George Michaels, the New Hampshire auctioneer and appraiser, spent two days with us. Auctioneer William Josko, of Fairfield, Connecticut, not only taught us well but actually opened up his books to us."

No matter how good a professional course is, the new auctioneer must still chart his personal course to establish consignment, as well as buying customer contacts. He must make decisions about whether to buy or stick to consignments (Don Saltzman leans toward at least partial ownership), whether to concentrate on a particular geographic locale or not. The car-related collections owned by Don and Carol and Sheila included many manuscripts, jewelry, and other items, which crossed several collecting categories. This gave them a good lead-in to potential consignors for other types of manuscript, autograph, jewelry, and toy collectibles. Thus, their first auctions had a nice mixture but still hung together.

If not everything consigned to them during the trial period was of prime desirability, they recognized and accepted this as part of the growing process. As for free-lancing rather than having a permanent space, they have not ruled out the latter but feel they have to test their market over a more extended period before making that kind of commitment. The biggest problems they have encountered as free-lance roving auctioneers are local ordinances and nuisance problems thrown in their way by some people doing "regular" business in the area where the auction is scheduled to take place. The free-lance auction eliminates decisions about reserves (see Glossary). Merchandise must be moved out at the end of the sale, so, except for small things that can be packed into a station wagon, these types of auctions tend to be unreserved.

Another auctioneer, R. Joseph Cameron, of South Windsor, Connecticut, who switched from the chemical business to full-time free-lance auctioneering, is known as "the no-nonsense auctioneer." His career switch was by no means a sudden one; even while his working life still centered on chemicals, all his spare time was devoted to auctiongoing and learning about the antiques business.

While attending an auction one evening, he was asked to fill in when one of the runners didn't show up. This led to a permanent part-time job, which incorporated being a furniture loader, relief auctioneer, floor helper, truck loader — anything connected with setting up and conducting the auction. By the time he was ready to strike out on his own, Mr. Cameron had had ample opportunity to learn all the do's and don't's of the business. He also had a clear perspective about the work and the pitfalls that lurk behind the show-biz image of the auction scene. Anyone who wants to earn enough to support a family that includes three children, as he does, should, according to Mr. Cameron, be prepared to:

1. Make a solid capital investment or else find a backer. "Few moneylenders, including the Small Business Administration, are anything but reluctant to advance money to this type of operation."

2. Be on call twenty-four hours a day, seven days a week, to follow up on any and all opportunities to buy.

3. Be a direct seller or door pounder. "Your product is yourself, and you must go directly to doctors, lawyers, estate executors, bankers, et cetera, who will not be interested in doing business over the phone until they get to know you."

4. Be a civic-organization and church-group joiner, doer, helper. Offering to assist at charitable events in your professional capacity is the sort of good-will building that leads to word-of-mouth recommendations.

5. Figure your profits carefully before taking on a sale or "giving" on a commission. An estate should be at least $10,000 to warrant your veering from the standard 20 percent. If you have too many sales that gross you $5000, you should rethink your business, since you are then in the marginal category.

6. Be sure to make allowances in your overhead costs for advertising, and do so with steadily increasing rates in mind. Don't rely on

just one kind of medium, either. Dollar for dollar, the antiques section of the Newtown *Bee* probably does the most for Cameron Auctions because buyers from New York as well as New England read it. However, the Hartford and Springfield papers are important, too. The latter comes out twice a day, so that means two ads.

7. The advertising budget must also allow for announcement fliers — with pictures, if it's a good estate. Fliers about your business in general, rather than specific sales, should also be sent to bankers, lawyers, dealers, and collectors, to keep the company's name always in front of them.

Mr. Cameron has no plans to alter his mom-and-pop (Mrs. Cameron keeps the books) roving-auctioneer status; he has encountered no problems in hiring places like the Knights of Columbus Hall at very reasonable rates. He would like to build up his schedule from fifteen sales a year to twenty-five. This would enlarge the business enough to support two generations; one sixteen-year-old son already helps out with some auctioneering.

SAME PLACE–SAME TIME AUCTIONEERS

To the five colleges in and near the town of Amherst, Massachusetts, one should perhaps add the Amherst Auction Galleries. It has been the school of hard knocks for several other people in this book. Meg and Bruce Cummings observed and studied its comings and goings while tending the food concession; Peter Rakelbusch was a runner here, as was Mark Polon, whom we shall meet a bit later. Added to these Amherst four, there is gallery-owner Bill Hubbard's own son, Chris, who has come into the business, and a retired partner's daughter who is the official bookkeeper.

Bill Hubbard himself is a Harvard graduate who began collecting and dealing in antiques while still a high school teacher, and "when the good stuff was unquestionably at its best in terms of getting it. Being a dealer was good, but auctions are better. I do a million dollars' worth of business a year, which makes for a nice business, and I want to keep it just that big . . . and that small. I don't have any need or want to be Parke Bernet."

The gallery amply illustrates the advantages of having a permanent site in a town where you are well connected with the banking as well as the antiques and collecting community. The regularly scheduled Saturday morning auctions are as much a social as a business event. Bill estimates about 20 percent of his audiences to be dealers, and these can be seen trading gossip as well as making deals and bidding.

Once the auction begins, lots are moved at a steady, brisk pace, although not nearly as fast as at a large city auction. Since there are no catalogues, the auctioneer takes more time to describe each offering. The minute an item is sold, the runners or floor men deliver it to the buyer. No mystery here about who bought what. Merchandise is for the most part consigned and unreserved, but just as the atmosphere is relaxed, so are the rules in this regard. In spite of the substantial nature of the gallery's business, the overhead is not any higher than it would be for someone just starting out. Except for Bill and Chris, everyone, including the bookkeeper, is hired on a freelance basis, for the time of the auction, at basic hourly wages.

I asked Bill Hubbard how he felt about some of his former assis-

Inspection time at the Amherst Auction Galleries takes place Friday night and on Saturday morning before the sale begins.

tants striking out on their own, especially with competing auction businesses. He shrugged philosophically, yet when he said that in hiring people "you try to look for more Indians than chiefs," he was obviously thinking of his erstwhile runner Mark Polon, whose evening auction in the neighboring town of Greenfield I was scheduled to attend that night.

Mark Polon brings to mind people who, with more hearsay than firsthand knowledge, liken auctioneering to Broadway show business and envision the auctioneer as a cross between a Texas cowboy and a movie actor. Mark has the tall, rangy good looks that might fit either role. Actually this "colonel" (a title country-style auctioneers often adopt) is really a "doctor," with a Ph.D. in psychology from the University of Massachusetts. To help defray his tuition costs, he went to work for Bill Hubbard, and because teaching positions in psychodrama — his first career choice — became very scarce, he decided to pursue auctioneering full time. Like Hubbard, he chose to work within the framework of a regular time and place. He rents rather than owns his place, and his auctions are on Saturday nights instead of Saturday mornings.

Bill Hubbard and his son Chris usually split auctioneering duties in half, though both remain at the block throughout.

Mark considers his experience as a runner for the Amherst Auction Galleries priceless. "It was from Bill Hubbard that I learned to throw out the invitation for the first bid in order to tell the retail customer the price I think the item should fetch, working backward from there. I also learned to do appraisals and the whole mechanics of organizing the sale."

The experience as a student of psychodrama and psychology is not considered wasted at all: "I see an auction very much like theater. When I get up there, things are never predictable and I have to get in touch with the audience. If things get too noisy, I speak very low so people have to shut up to hear me. If things get sluggish, I raise my voice to wake them up. There's also the whole business of making eye contact; it's all psychology."

As for the behind-the-scenes functions — going out to get business, setting up, unpacking, paying out checks, donning a three-piece suit to visit bankers, and keeping in contact with the community through his businessmen's-association and historical-society

Auctioneer Mark Polon (dark sweater and light pants) grabs a few minutes of relaxation while he can.

memberships — Mark accepts all as pieces that make up an overall lifestyle he likes because every day and every task is different.

I couldn't help wondering about Mark's need to compete with his firmly entrenched old boss. Mark admitted, "It *is* hard being new, even without competition, but I feel I've built up my own special interest in Victoriana as opposed to Amherst's emphasis on Americana, and the fact that we have different hours sets us apart further. Besides, things seem to be falling into place. When I started out two years ago, I made a five-year business plan that included moving to a bigger place — which I just did — and doing regular auctions, which I'm doing."

My talk with Mark preceded his first Saturday night auction in a new building. By the time the first lot was brought out, the hall was solidly packed. Bidding was lower than at the Amherst auction, but it was steady. Many of the people here had been at the morning auction. There were more runners, and three bookkeepers rather than one. Whether this auction will hit a stride of a million-dollar business or falter, or perhaps go up, up, and away, only time and the owner's perseverance will tell.

SPECIALTY AUCTIONEERS

Just as auctioneers take the less than spectacular lots with the crème de la crème in order to maintain steady sales schedules, so those who specialize are usually generalists as well, at the same time building up a reputation for particular specialty auctions as much as possible. Even an auctioneer without a reputation for jewelry or paintings or tools, to give some examples, eagerly seeks out merchandise that lends itself to being featured in specialty sales, because the public seems to respond to these with great enthusiasm.

Sometimes the specialty is not so much the type of consignment as the type of consignor; to wit, the celebrity auction, featuring objects as esoteric as the eyelashes from the estate of the late movie actress Joan Crawford. For newcomers to the highly competitive New York auction scene, like Plaza Galleries, such auctions provide invaluable television and press exposure.

There are those who have been able to build highly profitable auction businesses by adhering at all times to a selected category. Two of the best-known impresarios in this line are Charles Hamilton and George Lowrey, both operating in New York City. Hamilton is probably the foremost dealer in autographs in the country, and his auctions held in the Waldorf Astoria Hotel draw dealers and collectors from near and far. Lowrey's Swann Gallery is the scene of weekly auctions, considered *the* place to find out what's going on in the specialized world of books and manuscripts.

Specialization may extend to the actual method of organizing and conducting the auction. Here the mail order auction serves as a fascinating illustrative phenomenon and George Rinsland, of Allentown, Pennsylvania, a triumphant archetype. What started as a mimeographed list has grown into four annotated and illustrated catalogues a year, mailed to several thousand paying subscribers and grossing as much as $300,000 a year. The auctions star political Americana, though auctioneer Rinsland has sold furniture. His biggest sale was a painting that went for $8500 on a drop shipment arrangement, meaning that it got listed without leaving the consignor's home and was shipped directly to the bidder. The more typical sale runs to $40 to $50, with many $5 and $6 items as well.

What differentiates the mail order auction catalogue from the mail order sales catalogues, described in Chapter 3? The latter feature specific prices but no ordering deadlines; the former have estimated value estimates but specific deadlines. The risk that the consignor and the mail order auctioneer take is that there will be either no bids or bids that are too low. Rinsland has overcome this problem by an interesting method of allowing the highest bidder to buy the item at a price slightly higher than the second highest bid. (For example, if the highest bid is $20, the second highest is $10, the buyer pays $11 rather than his bidding price of $20.) In addition, Rinsland does allow occasional reserves. He does cite yet another occasional risk; namely, shaky credit since so many bidders are individuals and small dealers.

The mail order auction is not for anyone seeking lots of person-to-person contact. If the Rinsland auctions are used as a yardstick, however, the financial rewards can be considerable, and it should thus come as no surprise that similar ventures have been started by others, some with auctioneer-published price guides, which are sold through the auction catalogues (see Chapter 8, Spinoffs, on self-publishing options).

What does it take to get started as a mail order auctioneer?

Not surprisingly, George Rinsland attributes his success to lots of reading in order to become knowledgeable, and willingness to cope with an incredible number of details. His retirement in 1972 from, you guessed it, the postal service, and the subsequent buildup of the Americana auctions, were preceded by years of self-education. "I started back in nineteen sixty-four, knowing nothing. When I bought a document signed S. L. Clemens, I had no idea what it was, but I had heard of Charles Hamilton in New York and so I wrote to him. He offered to buy it but I decided to do some more research, and that's what I continued to do with other antiques and collectibles I bought."

Today he does no personal buying at all, but he needs his knowledge to judge consignments. He asks people to send descriptions and pictures to avoid undue shipping, "but a lot of my consignors are dealers and they just pack things up and send them to me. This is all part of being willing to handle detail. People do pay for shipping things back, but, still, I have to unpack everything, look at it, pack it up again . . . The catalogue itself is even more detail work." George does it all, with the help of his wife and a typist. He cautions anyone contemplating this type of business to give himself or herself plenty of time to get out the catalogue and thus take advantage of bulk rates. "I send my catalogues out a month and a half before the auction date."

For George Rinsland, the move to the customer side of the post office window has definitely been a satisfying and profitable one.

THE TAG SALE SPECIALIST

Every group has its pecking order. Among those who dispose of other people's personal property, the auction houses have clearly staked out the top position for themselves, and those who do tag sales right in people's own homes are generally considered at the bottom. Yet many a tag sale business that started for pin money or fun has transformed housewives into entrepreneurs whose earnings have sent many kids through college, and then some. Originally, a tag or garage sale was a homeowner's way of cleaning out a batch of household goods no longer needed, as part of spring cleaning or before moving or when someone died. As more and more women with a sense of what things were worth and a flair for organization offered home owners a hassle-free, theft-protected sale at prices that more than offset the organizer's fee, the tag sale grew into a real business.

In spite of rising competition, success stories continue to unfold. Some of the more astute tag salers have taken courses in antiques to help them better to appraise and price and advertise salient feature items. As a result, the humble tag sale has been known to fetch prices close to, and at times on a par with, what the owners would obtain at auction.

Some tag sales are advertised in antiques publications, with ads that read much like those for auctions. Still, the sales announced by posters tacked to telephone poles and ads in local throwaway papers remain popular, too. Tag sale organizers with auctioneering licenses are becoming common, as are those who open consignment shops, where people with less than a houseful of merchandise can leave things. The owner of a consignment shop takes a 40 percent commission (50 percent in some parts of the country), as opposed to the 20 percent tag sale fee. At the same time, many antique shops also put up signs that say WE DO TAG SALES.

To differentiate themselves from the "pin money" tag salers, the bigger companies put a minimum on what they will handle — anywhere from $3000 to $7000. Minimums don't always work out, according to one Westport, Connecticut, tag saler, Irene Marcenaro: "People have a way of removing some of the things you see during an estimate . . . but then you usually get more money than you estimate, and this evens things out. It's a good business."

ESTATE LIQUIDATORS

To give the home sale business further éclat, there is the liquidation sale, which can take a variety of forms. One is the estate sale, which is pretty much a tag sale by a classier name, and there is also a more lavish version of the estate sale, which may not even be held on the owner's property.

As the name implies, the estate or liquidation specialist aims for big things. Contacts for merchandise are made with bankers, estate executors, funeral directors, and so forth. A liquidation sale may entail a mailing and large illustrated ads. Promotion-minded planners have been known to arrange special art exhibits as a corollary to a prestigious sale. This can be a sale-exhibit or just an exhibit, to make extra money or as a means of building good will in the community.

The tag saler who expands may lean toward running consignment shops and very occasionally holding auctions. When the estate liquidator gets into establishing a real estate base, the shop is more likely to be a large warehouse, which doubles as a retail shop and auction house and is aimed at attracting decorators and dealers as much as private customers. The more successful estate warehouses have antiques specialists on their payroll and can gross in the same million-dollar range as the Amherst Auction Galleries — in short, big but not too big. Fee appraisals are often co-existing activities, especially for those liquidators who do not own their own warehouses.

The money being made in home sales has not escaped the large auction houses, many of whom have themselves gone into the house sale business. Sotheby's PB Eighty-Four has been running an advertising campaign in small-town weeklies, heretofore the tag sale advertiser's bailiwick. The ads carry such headlines as: GARAGE SALES AREN'T FOR ANTIQUES . . . An interesting social commentary on tag-liquidation sales: the tag sale business, which, though profitable, remains at the bottom of the prestige scale, is predominantly run by women. The liquidation sales field, and most auctioneering, is predominantly male-run. There are exceptions and mom-and-pop situations, but the facts remain.

THE SHOW PROMOTER

We see the antiques show as a three-dimensional form of communication — an extension of two-dimensional forms such as
publishing.
— Nat Mager, Publisher, *New York State Law Journal;*
Director, National Antiques and Arts Festival

We have already discussed the show as a major segment of the
dealer's market picture. Those who organize the shows represent the
missing link in this story. Actually, other types of impresarios like
the auctioneer have much more in common with the dealer than does
the show promoter, since they are dependent on knowledgeability
in identifying and evaluating antiques and collectibles. Their ultimate profit is realized from the sale of merchandise.

The show promoter's role and profit structure are quite different:
his gross earnings derive from the total money received from exhibitors for rentals and show visitors for entry tickets. The net profit is
the sum remaining after advertising, promotion, rental, and other
costs incurred in the show's productions are deducted.

Although coordinating and promotional, rather than buying and
selling, abilities must be the promoter's strongest suit, being a show
dealer is one of the best ways to obtain inside knowledge of how
other promoters work, the dealers' needs, and the customers' responses. Perhaps that is why, if you scratch many a promoter, you
will uncover an erstwhile and, in many instances, a still-existing
dealer.

Usually the dealer-promoter contents himself with a few size-con-
trolled productions per annum, though dollar success cannot always
be measured strictly according to quantity. It is safe to assume that
promoters with lineups of thirty or more shows a year are doing
more than reasonably well, but some of the most successful long-
time promoters earn sufficient returns from two to fourteen regularly
scheduled shows.

In terms of the bottom line, "quality control" is a question of
attitude and personal taste, and flea markets cannot be ignored. Besides, there are flea markets and flea markets. The three weekend
flea markets at Brimfield, Massachusetts, where dealers from all over

the country stock up on inventory for the coming year, have been successful business enterprises, first for founder Gordon Reid and, since his death, for his daughters and their families. Many flea markets do, of course, deteriorate in terms of their connection with antiques and collectibles. However, this shift in emphasis to food and other staples, with only a smattering of good old things, is not unprofitable for the promoters.

Five Basic Determinants for Successful Show Promotion

The rewards that have attracted so many into show promotion also make this an immensely competitive field. And so, before you launch into your own promotion, be sure you understand what the promoters interviewed for this chapter regard as the five basics for success:

1. Financing
2. Scheduling
3. Slanting and balancing
4. Handling rules and regulations
5. Creativity

FINANCING   There are three methods of financing a show. The first is to have a charity sponsor the show and share in the profits. The second is to underwrite it all yourself. The third is to make an arrangement with a large corporate type of organization, which in effect hires the promoter as a manager and assumes all financial risks.

Irene Stella has built her ten-year career as one of the most respected show promoters in the state of New Jersey on a judicious mixture of all three methods. "It was the charity-related show that really got me started. I had retired from retail fashion promotion to raise seven kids. When a local woman's club to which I belonged ran an antiques show, I felt something was wrong because they drew one hundred and eighty-five people but only made three hundred and ten dollars. The following year I ran the show for them, as a volunteer. and they got two hundred people and made two thousand dollars and forty-nine cents."

When word of this got around, other clubs and organizations began to call Irene for information. Eventually she went into business, concentrating most of her initial energies in the area of charity show promotion. Her method of handling charity show finances has worked so well that it has been widely copied by other promoters. Quite simply, she reserves the money paid by the exhibitors to cover expenses for table rentals, ads, contracts, and her own profits. The charity assumes financial responsibility for the building and provides the labor, which would normally have to be paid for, in exchange for money taken in at the gate. All this is clearly set forth in a form sent to interested organizations and reprinted herewith.

In the second method of show financing, the promoter shoulders all financial and manpower burdens. (Cash outlays for rentals can be decreased by working out an arrangement whereby the owner of the facility takes a share of the take, but most promoters don't look too favorably on this method.) In this case, promotion and other work usually handled by organization volunteers must be done by the promoter or hired help. The theory behind this financing is that all or most of the exhibitor fees will go to expenses, and the gate will be reserved as the promoter's profit. Promoters say it doesn't always add up quite this way and that it takes a big show, with an absolute minimum of fifty dealers and a reasonably high entry fee, to keep the bottom line black.

For a promoter who plans a show in the heart of a big city like New York, this type of financing involves even higher stakes. According to Nat Mager, "The union problems alone can be fantastic. The electricity at the Park Avenue Armory is twelve thousand dollars." Mr. Mager feels he has an enormous advantage in running his shows from beneath a year-round corporate umbrella, which provides both financing and staff from business activities not connected with the shows.

If you are not part of a large organization, your third financial choice is to enlist a corporation to provide the backing or the building, while you provide the name and talent. This is how Irene Stella handles the shows she puts on at the New Jersey Meadowlands complex. There are all sorts of variations to the fee arrangements, as she explained, from a straight fee to a fee plus profit sharing.

PROVISIONS FOR ANTIQUE SHOWS

Director Provides

All plans, exhibits, arrangements and advertising needed for a successful Antique Show, Fair or Flea Market, that is:

1) Agreed number of exhibitors. (a minimum of 40)

2) Contracts and mailing.

3) Printing of tickets & posters, dealer signs, tags, area signs, etc.

4) Distribution of tickets and posters to dealers. (Approx. 3,000 tickets & 100 posters.)

5) Advertising to trade magazines, local papers and publications, paid ads and free listings, submitted to at least 8 papers.

6) Large signs or banners.

7) Needed articles, such as tables, electrical equipment, etc.

8) Workable floor plan and implementation.

Organization Provides

1) Suitable site or building and any expenses incurred in acquiring or maintaining same, such as rentals, insurance, or custodial fees.

2) Publicity chairmen to type & mail news releases to all papers, and perform all duties needed to benefit show.

3) Design and execution of one poster (black ink on white paper 11" x 17") to be used for printing tickets & posters.

4) Distribution of tickets and posters to friends and local shops.

5) Members to collect admission charge at the door, during the show.

6) Food and beverage for sale. Rest room facilities all hours of set up and show.

7) Adequate help for set up, breakdown and clean up.

All dealers fees are used to pay for director's responsibilities, including director's fee. In this way the director is free to properly provide for the success of the show and the organization incurs no bills or expenses. The entire gate is clear profit for the organization.

This is the form promoter Irene Stella gives to charity organizations so that everyone understands his and her respective responsibilities.

SCHEDULING   One of the most crucial decisions facing the promoter is where and when to schedule shows. The ideal location is the one that draws and accommodates a maximum number of dealers and visitors comfortably and safely. A large crowd, in itself, is not necessarily a good crowd. Dealers want people who have money and are interested in buying, not just looking. Accessibility to highways, parking, and public transportation are important factors. Since the true success of a show lies in its becoming a regularly scheduled event, the foresighted promoter checks on the possibility of an option to re-lease a site. If you rent a place for a weekly flea market–type show, options to re-lease as well as sublet are worth securing. These will enable you to keep a good thing going or get out of something that's not working, as the case may be. And always make a careful check of other show schedules. There is no trade organization, but promoters recognize the benefits of cooperating in order to avoid conflicts.

The matter of scheduling also involves setting up one's calendar for the year. A schedule may be too full or too light. A particular show within a set circuit may require some re-thinking by the promoter as to location. For J. Jordan Humberstone, his own state of Michigan provides just enough of a market for the seven shows to which he wants to confine his management activities. The market is uniform enough for all the shows to be of the same general nature. Diane Wendy, who started as a secretary–girl Friday with the oldest show management company in the business — Nuttall-Bostwick, now generally known as Westchester Enterprises — spreads her fourteen annual shows over four states. These range from the prestigious Park Avenue Antiques Show to several flea markets and outdoor antiques fairs run under the auspices of charity organizations. If a show becomes too expensive to make a profit, like one formerly held at the New York Coliseum, it is dropped.

SLANTING AND BALANCING   By slanting shows to particular trends and interests — nostalgia, miniatures, photographica, advertising, glass, and so forth — many promoters have built up a clientele of both exhibitors and strong buying audiences. These "theme" shows are usually smaller and easier to target in terms of advertising and promotion. Several large promoters who suggested this as the best route for a beginner also expressed interest in doing more specialized shows themselves.

Within the large general show, a promoter with a sense of balance can create several smaller shows; he can group all dealers within a certain category in one section. Balance must also come into play if you want to avoid a show that is top-heavy with a particular type of merchandise. This may involve some risk-taking if you turn away dealers, but successful promoters feel the risk pays off through satisfied dealers and customers.

HANDLING RULES AND REGULATIONS   If more people considered legal agreements and announcements of rules as tools for obviating problems rather than as adversary measures, there would be far fewer arguments than result from handshake agreements.

A good dealer contract leaves no unanswered questions as to set-up and take-down time, union regulations, display specifications. The more problems you anticipate, the fewer you will encounter. Use contracts from other shows as takeoff points, combine the best points from all, then add your own — and then check out the contract with a lawyer, to be safe. Irene Stella feels that a good dealer contract, combined with a covering letter that fills in specifics about rules, requirements, and available appointments for a particular show, is the best tool a new promoter can use to solicit exhibitors. She applies the principle of spelling out things clearly to all her dealings with other people. In addition to the provisions about general responsibilities and profit sharing for a charity-run show, she provides the organizations with specific rules and suggestions to help those organizations carry out their publicity responsibilities. (See Part II, Resources, for help on publicity.)

CREATIVITY   Besides all the "musts" that go into a well-coordinated show, there are all the creative extras that build your reputation as a true impresario.

What special attraction will draw the most jaded showgoer, or attract the tag-along who isn't really interested in antiques? One of Nat Mager's widely imitated innovations was a special separate coin section as part of the Madison Square Garden Antiques Show. This has been expanded to include all sorts of paper memorabilia. Appraisers and appraisers' groups are another popular show attraction. The fee for the appraisers is usually paid by the promoter (around $500 a day), with the appraisal fees donated to a charity.

Irene Stella has found a big circus band organ both a popular and a useful attraction: it helps direct cars to the gate. The interest in fix-it booths, where specialists in repairs and restoration sell their services and know-how rather than merchandise, led Irene to assemble an entire fix-it–show-within-a-show, and this new wrinkle in show promotion is sure to be found in other show enterprises.

Finally, there is creative problem solving and anticipating. Here again, Irene Stella serves as an examplar. Whereas the management usually stays pretty well behind the scenes, Irene and her helpers can be found right out front, ready to answer questions from visitors and dealers alike.

No one has to look for the promoter at a Stella show: Irene and several helpers are at a desk right out front, directing traffic, answering questions, and, if they arise, complaints.

CHAPTER 6

❖ ❖ ❖

Artisans and
Technologists

Some antique objects survive years of use or display in good or even mint condition. Others, like the famous Altai Carpet from the Hermitage Museum in Russia, survive as a matter of fortuitous circumstance. This valuable ancient textile would long since have decayed into a fragment at best, had not some robbers scavenged the grave in which it was buried. The thieves made off with the precious metals and stones and left the rug behind, along with an unsealed opening, which allowed rain to seep in. The rain froze, encasing the rug in a perfect state of preservation.

Not all antiques, even those of much more recent vintage, fare as well. Fine wood finishes are covered with layers of paint and shellac by people unattuned to the beauty of the original. Fabrics, paintings, and books are subject to stress or poor climatic conditions. With the application of some knowledgeable and skillful fixing up or, if need be, very complex restoration, these objects can become once again useful and possibly even valuable. Because old things are harder and more expensive to obtain all the time, the fixers and restorers are much in demand and are in fact becoming promotable attractions

— as already evidenced by Irene Stella's featuring special areas for fix-it practitioners as part of her antiques and collectibles shows.

TRAINING AND EDUCATION FOR RESTORERS AND CONSERVATORS

The very finest restorers are scientists as well as artisans, using laboratory and technological skills to analyze exactly what matter and material are present in an object, and the effect on it of time, environment, and other chemical processes. This analytical knowledge determines the choice of repair materials and processes.

The conservator is the equivalent in art and antiques of the doctor practicing preventive medicine. The top-level conservator is a consultant who advises a client how to deal with a particular problem, care for the object, and restore it. The actual restoration work may be entrusted to an artisan working under the conservator's guidance. The conservator's workplace is a highly sophisticated laboratory, with tools and equipment varying from category to category of specialization. The conservator's technical expertise makes him something of an art and antiques detective, so he is often called on to ascertain authenticity — something of an overlap with the appraisal profession.

The way in which restorers and conservators learn their trade has changed considerably over the years. At one time, knowledge was handed down in the apprenticeship tradition, often from father to son. Today, apprenticeship has given way to adult education and college courses and how-to-do-it books. For those primarily interested in earning a living as an artisan, these serve as a sound base. (See Part II, Resources, for the address of the American Crafts Council as a guide to specific programs.)

The restorer-conservator with an eye to a position with a museum or a consulting firm needs a good mastery of the biological sciences and will do well to investigate college- or museum-affiliated programs in conservation science. Programs differ in their basic orientation: the State University program at Oneonta, New York, has a graduate program that concentrates on painting conservation; the

New York University Institute of Fine Arts Conservation Center, in New York City, directs most of its energies toward the technical aspects of conservation; the Henry Francis du Pont Winterthur Museum program, run under the auspices of the University of Delaware, covers the decorative arts and general conservation. There are other interesting mergers, such as the interdisciplinary program of the Center for Material Research in Archeology and Ethnology with a central laboratory at the Massachusetts Institute of Technology.

Outside the United States, conservation programs are given at Queen's University in Kingston, Ontario, Canada; the Institute of Archeology and the Courtauld Institute of Art of the University of London; the Doerner Institute in Munich, Germany; the Institut Royal du Patrimoine Artistique in Brussels, Belgium; and the Instituto Centrale del Restauro in Rome, Italy.

A more broad-based preservation interest is that which concerns itself with the preservation of historic buildings and neighborhoods. Opportunities here cross educational boundaries. One example is the summer intern program sponsored by the National Trust for Historic Preservation (see People and Places in Part II, Resources) which draws on students in architectural history, architecture, art history, economics, history, horticulture, the humanities, journalism, landscape architecture, law, library sciences, maritime-related studies, and planning.

THE ECONOMIC PERSPECTIVE

Whether your interests lie in repair or fixing or fine restoration work, the opportunities for profits are very real. In the furniture field particularly, short-cut refinishers or strippers have earned tidy incomes developing systems that are, in turn, sold as franchises to small businesses. Not all the franchisers are concerned with preservation of fine patinas; many use the stripping system for ordinary pieces not worthy of hand-finishing processes. Thus, the quick-strip type of restoration business is one way for a small business person to make a living with or without the organizational support of a franchise. The more managerially oriented may want to set up an independent organization, becoming the one who sells rather than buys the franchise.

Some Furniture Refinishers

Robert Berra, of Hadley, Masschusetts, has a small business that combines a nationally manufactured stripping system and fine hand restoration. His shop has a large rear work area that comfortably accommodates the dipping and stripping operation. The front of the shop contains the pieces he works on by hand, the kinds of things to which he plans eventually to devote all his energies. The firm name, Metamorphosis, aptly symbolizes not just the transformation Bob Berra can effect in a creaky and gook-covered chair, but the metamorphosis of his own lifestyle — from chairman of the board of a major international corporation to financial administrator at the University of Massachusetts to restorer.

Leo and Rayanna Schmuecker, of Bethel, Connecticut, also bought a furniture-stripping system. They opted for a franchise setup run by a Tennesseean named Bixenman. After several years, the Schmueckers, feeling that Mr. Bix, as he was known, was not making the most of a very good thing, became sales representatives for the franchise. Eventually, they bought out the original owner. Bix is still the name used on shops now part of an extensive franchise network. The management includes two Schmuecker sons.

Whatever the hand restorer's opinion of these very modernized short-cut businesses that cater as much, if not more, to secondhand furniture dealers and refinishing hobbyists as to those in antiques — for a number of small shop owners, as well as other Bix-type franchise companies, the financial rewards are real and important.

Quilt Repair and Restoration

If I seem to be dwelling on furniture refinishing, this is only because so many people are and can be involved in this area, at many different levels. Glass is another category calling for the services of many "doctors," who can mend broken pieces, fill in knicks, and touch up chips.

The relatively recent quilt-collecting boom and the appreciation evinced by museums in quilts as fine art have given rise to a fairly narrow speciality, antique quilt fabric replacement. Pie Galinat is a practitioner of this craft. She started out to become an artist but hated art school, and, to bide time until she decided on another career, she went to work for an antique shop specializing in quilts. The shop, Kelter-Malce, besides being conveniently located near Pie's apartment in New York's Greenwich Village, also served to trigger renewed appreciation for a Connecticut childhood in a house filled with old things, including her grandmother's fine needlework.

When things were slow in the shop, Pie, being pretty handy with fabric and thread, began to repair imperfect quilts. At the end of two years she realized that, as big as the city of New York was, there seemed no one else there doing fabric replacements. What's more, since all the big collectors and dealers had at one point or another been in the shop, Pie knew them all and they were familiar with her work. This open market, and her contacts in it, seemed an invitation to her to turn her job into an independent business, which could be run right from her apartment.

Pie did some advertising in New England antiques papers but found her New York market was big enough to keep her busy. Her advertising is currently limited to local antiques fairs and the Museum of Folk Art's quarterly magazine, *The Clarion*. This very limited promotional expense is her only overhead. Her supplies consist of old printed cottons she has collected over the years and which she is able to supplement through a "pen pal," who sends her packages of goodies whenever she comes across something.

With the help of a friend, Don Self, she has added a nicely profitable sideline to the quilt-repair business; namely, customized stretcher bars onto which quilts, edged at the back with Velcro, are mounted for display. Even this calls for time and precision, since the old quilt's natural tendency to be off an inch or so at one side makes it necessary to hand-sew the Velcro.

The continuing popularity of quilts promises to keep Pie Galinat's quilt fabric replacement service going and growing. She's hoping for enough of a lull to devote some time toward creating her own original contemporary quilts. She believes strongly that this is a thriving craft and that today's quilts — especially the original designs — will very definitely become tomorrow's coveted antiques.

The same interest in quilts that has given rise to the need for people like Pie has turned the attention of other specialists to the care and cleaning of quilts. One such noted quilt authority, Patsy Orlofsky, has started to launch a conservatory workshop in South Salem, New York, to service museum-quality quilts as well as rare fabrics, rugs, tapestries, and costumes. Pie Galinat's more limited area of activity will be incorporated within this grander scheme of things.

GETTING IT ALL TOGETHER: A CLEARING HOUSE OF ARTISAN AND TECHNOLOGICAL SERVICES

Ken Linsner is a very dedicated young man.

He is dedicated to the well-being of works of art and antiquity and to this end has both studied and taught at the N.Y.U. Fine Arts

Pie Galinat's interest in quilts was nurtured by the grandmother who made this handsome Log Cabin quilt block for a pillow. Pie's friend Don Self framed it in a handmade Tramp Art frame.

Pie Galinat performing some of her quilt-replacement magic.

Conservation Center, worked on ancient excavations abroad, and served as a specialist in Egyptology at the Brooklyn Museum. His particular expertise as a conservator and restorer is in the area of paper.

Ken Linsner is also dedicated to achieving his long-range objective of setting up a clearinghouse for a broad spectrum of services that will include conservation, restoration, appraisal, brokerage, collector consultation, fine photography of collections, and anything else the corporate or private collector might need and want. He sees this objective as a way of surpassing the earnings of museum positions (about $25,000 a year) or even the considerably better $40-an-hour rate earned by well-established free-lance conservators.

Ken's partner in this grand design is a former fellow student, Ellen Epstein. Under their corporate name, Art Restoration & Conservation, Ken and Ellen have advertised in such media as the *New York Times, Barron's,* and *Antiques* magazine, as well as small local papers. They have also taken booths at interior design shows to demonstrate conservation methods. The partners have not let their ultimate goal interfere with smaller and more immediate opportunities.

Their very first client was a suburban woman who wanted to have an old milk can antiqued. "She got a true bargain; we asked a friend who has since become a well-known painter to paint and sign the can." This concept of subcontracting is at the heart of their operation. No two people could possibly handle the variety of restoration and conservation projects they solicit. "The whole idea," as Ken sees it, "is to eliminate the little black book of restorers' addresses by creating a one-stop personalized clearinghouse where someone can be sure of getting a qualified person to handle any problem." The advantage to the restorer or any other expert who works with them? "One large organization to pull a lot of little people doing little things together."

THE "NEW" ARTISANS

From a semantic point of view the distinction between the designation "antiques" and "crafts" is largely one of time. Both center on handcrafted objects, but whereas antiques embrace 6000 years of creativity, the term crafts is usually applied to the output of one era. The antiques *and* crafts explosion in the late 1960s arose out of a need people felt to personalize and revitalize their increasingly automated and monotonous surroundings and lifestyles. Collecting from the past provided one type of creative and meaningful outlet; relearning and practicing old skills, another.

The interest in antiques grew and expanded to include not only the very old handmade objects, but the machine-made products of more happily remembered industrial times. The crafts movement also grew and expanded. Along with the "new" traditional crafts artisan, a whole new breed of artist-craftsmen and women was spawned. It is their often dramatic and jolting interpretation of traditional skills that has given birth to an entire new "circa" (see Glossary) of contemporary crafts.

The more forward-looking collectors have already heeded the handwriting on the wall and taken advantage of the opportunity to collect from living artists, maintaining easily collected provenance records of the genre in general and of the artists in particular. As with anything collectible, there are both pedestrian and outstanding things, and it requires a developed taste and an understanding of what makes the circa unique to collect wisely. For example, fine hand-stitching may signify value and high quality for an antique quilt, but the contemporary collector would be wiser to use design originality as a criterion for collectibility and price worthiness.

As of this writing, contemporary crafts are still going through the "aging" process needed to make them acceptable to that segment of the public which is firmly convinced that old is better than new, at least in terms of investment. As someone who has moved back and forth between the antiques and the contemporary crafts worlds, both as a writer and as a collector, my feeling is that the crafts of the seventies, especially the creations of the Bicentennial, will take far less than a hundred or even fifty years to enter the art and antiques mainstream. In the meantime, restoration, combined with new and original designs or reproductions on a new and different scale, offer a sort of best-of-both-worlds approach. Let's see how this works out in actual practice.

*Contemporary quilt artists like Joan Schulze honor the tradition of the
past with splendidly fresh interpretations. "California," circa 1977.*
Photograph, S. Russie

Restoration Combined with New and Original Designs

Two former art teachers, Sue and Neil Connell, have turned the Clayton Store in Canaan, Connecticut, into a veritable "anything" restoration and re-creation business.

They do fine refinishing (no stripping), specializing in painted-finish furniture. They both restore or newly create grained, stenciled, and otherwise decorated surfaces. Their art background has enabled them to move into other areas, such as basket repair and reweaving. When working with tin and sheet iron, they not only repair but use old mirrors and discolored tin to design brand-new tin and mirrored sconces. Another favorite — old wallpapered hatboxes — also gets the old and new treatment; the Connells will make new lids with printed designs, match up missing patches, and also create original wallpapers. As if this weren't enough, they apply their old-new talents to the restoration of rooms in houses — graining and decorating woodwork, paneling, floors, picture frames — "just about anything that doesn't move."

Lest you think you need multimedia talents as an artisan to cater to the antiques lover, there is "the Stencil Lady," Pamela Friend, of Hanover, Massachusetts. Pamela's interest and professional involvement in this traditional form of wall decoration predates its almost fadlike popularity of recent years. She credits an aunt who was an artist with whetting her interest when she was a young girl, and a course in Early American Decoration taken at the Fletcher Farm Craft School, in Ludlow, Vermont, for conferring the needed skills.

According to Pamela, "Love of making things beautiful more than fast profits is what's needed to make a success in this profession. If you're willing to make a large investment in time — doing promotional lectures and demonstrations [see Chapter 8, Spinoffs] as well as actual work — and a reasonable investment in dollars [$50 to $4000 a year mostly in advertising] you can have a very interesting and comfortably profitable business."

Pamela loves tracking down old stencils, especially those discovered on walls in old houses, but she has also developed some very successful stencil designs of her own. To ease and enlarge the marketing of her work, she has stenciled a line of quilts, coverlets, and

"The Stencil Lady," Pamela Friend, with some favorite patterns.

curtains, which are sold through the showrooms and mail order catalogues of Constance Carol, Incorporated, of Plymouth and Lexington, Massachusetts. She advertises in a variety of media and has found the local free giveaways the ones that bring her the best response. Another antiques business owner told me that TV schedule giveway papers are also very good places to advertise.

Glass Paperweights: New Will Sell As Well As Old

Glass paperweights are the exception to the general rule that contemporary crafts are still awaiting acceptance by collectors.

Made only since the mid-nineteenth century, when curious glassmakers unraveled the method used in glass artifacts unearthed from some very ancient tombs, the small "new" glass forms immediately caught the public fancy. The mystery of how all those tiny glass rods got inside the clear glass casing, the function, and low cost, all made the paperweight the ideal souvenir collectible. In time, the paperweight craze diminished, and some of the factories that had been turning out editions of as many as 1000 copies of a design closed down. It took the efforts of a collector-distributor, Paul Jokelson, of Scarsdale, New York, to rekindle collecting enthusiasm, through the formation of the National Paperweight Collectors' Association.

The association's conventions have done much to spotlight leading glass artists and to spur new ones to penetrate the veil of mystery that continues to surround the craft. Those who manage to piece together the technique puzzle, and have the patience and skill, have no difficulty in marketing their weights through antiques shows, paperweight conventions, or through dealers eager to obtain selling franchises. Most glassmakers work in limited editions of approximately 300 weights, costing from $300 to $750 each. There are 3000 active collectors, and this helps to sustain the aura of exclusivity.

At twenty-two, Debbie Tarsitano, of Valley Stream, Long Island, is probably the youngest as well as the only female paperweight maker in the world. She has much in common with the dealer-turned-collector since her career as an artisan started just that way. In fact, Debbie's mother has taken over the dealership that Debbie and her dad began mostly to "buy better."

To begin at the beginning, Debbie's father, with her in tow, bought a weight for $5.00 at a local auction. This led both of them to a larger auction at Sotheby Parke Bernet, and before long they were so involved in collecting that they decided to become antiques show dealers. They learned about the contemporary artists and obtained a franchise from one to sell a certain number from each edition produced.

All this was, of necessity, part-time, because Mr. Tarsitano owns and runs a hardware store, and Debbie was still enrolled as an undergraduate art student at Hofstra University. Even before settling on her art major, she knew that it was the construction and design of paperweights that really held a deep and lasting interest for her. By the time graduation rolled around, Debbie had picked up the basics of paperweight techniques and was started on her full-time career goal of having her own glass studio to create a line of fine-quality paperweights. With the not inconsiderable help of her very handy

Debbie Tarsitano with some of her glass paperweights. Since the processes involved in weight making are jealously guarded, our camera was barred from Debbie's studio.

father, whom she hopes to have as a working partner once he retires, a studio has been furnished out of the Tarsitano garage. She has had some help from Paul Stankard, and other well-known designers ("you exchange one secret for another") and the Paperweight Collectors' Conventions have helped her to become known.

Debbie considers herself a beginner still — "I make three hundred weights a year and am satisfied with only forty" — but is at the same time confident of her future. This confidence has been boosted by a chance to display one of her designs in the Corning Glass Museum and by the personal interest taken in her by one of the luminaries in the field, Scotland's Paul Ysart, who invited her to work with him in his studio. To make the separation easier for Mrs. Tarsitano, Ysart made her this offer: "Give me your daughter, and I'll give you one of my paperweights." In a field where the rewards for inside knowledge are high and coming by that knowledge is difficult, that's a pretty good offer.

The New Artisan in the Miniature-Collecting Market

There aren't too many doll houses left like the Palace, which fetched a handy $256,000 knockdown price at Christie's London auction rooms in 1978. There are, however, legions of collectors who, if they can't have or afford a "Titania's Palace," will bit by bit collect or make tiny treasures to fill their own dream houses. Their tastes run the gamut of architectural and furniture styles, with the most collectible and costly of the modern "minis" being the authentically scaled replicas of period pieces.

Not one other collecting category quite equals miniatures in their all-transcending appeal for do-it-yourself hobbyists, serious artisans, collectors — and all the people who have grabbed hold of the opportunity to serve their needs: publishers, show promoters, kit and tool manufacturers, and dealers. Though an indisputable part of the antiques-collectibles picture, miniatures constitute an industry distinct and apart. In the collectors' market of the future, the mass-manufactured kits and home hobbyist's creations may well take their place alongside such collectibles of the present as products manufactured in Occupied Japan, celluloid jewelry, and other "kitsch" delights. The carefully wrought miniatures created in the studios of those labeled "masters" do not have to await antique status to command collectors' prices. The collectors' veritable mania and the scarcity of antique miniatures aside, the scaled-down replicas of fine antique furniture, though not originals, are also not reproductions; the reduced scale carries its own form and authenticity. It is this, plus the skill involved, that commands prices of as much as $1700 for a single small piece.

Unlike the paperweight maker (there *are* makers of miniature paperweights!), the interested miniature artisan can find help from every conceivable source — magazines, books, workshops, and organizations. To sell one's wares, there are countless miniature collectors' shows, as well as antiques shows, antique and miniature supply shops that act as middlemen, and publications for selling by mail.

In San Francisco, John and Ellen Blauer, a couple who met and fell in love through miniature collecting, making, and dealing, run their combined businesses in a 101-year-old, twenty-two–room Victorian house. John attributes his lifelong fascination and appreciation of superior craftsmanship and microscopic detail to the influence of his father, a watchmaker. His early interest in miniature furniture and household accessories is the result of hearing his mother speak of her collection, which was destroyed in the 1906 earthquake and fire.

Since John's collecting long preceded the current craze, he was able to acquire several total collections and some 8000 individual Lilliputian treasures, for which he constructed a forty-two–room structure, called Maynard Manor. The collecting led to his own creation of fine-quality items to sell through his Miniature Mart. Ellen, in the meantime, started miniature making as an addendum to collecting and then turned to creating a line of miniatures for her mail order weaving supply business, the Peddler Shop, of Independence, Missouri. As she got more and more involved in miniatures, she created such firsts in the field as miniature wallpaper, miniature but authentic-looking collector plates, and Coca-Cola trays. She and John met by mail in 1966, married in 1973, and their combined businesses, located in San Francisco, now employ eleven full-time employees and many free-lance artists throughout the world.

In New York, yet another couple serves as a model to those interested in the career opportunities to be found in miniature artisanry and marketing. In the Tracy family, Foster (known as Tracy) is the "master" craftsman, though it is Mary Lee whose collecting passion started him off. As a child actress, playing in Lillian Hellman's *Children's Hour* in Chicago, Mary Lee discovered the Thorne Rooms in the Chicago Art Institute. Tracy started his business life with the New York Stock Exchange, but he had always enjoyed working with wood. He made a perfectly scaled little viola that actually played, and he would carry it around with him and show it to people in the shops that he visited with Mary Lee. They had no plans to get involved professionally, but after they visited some miniature shows, they decided to venture into miniaturing — selling Tracy's line of instruments and acting as agents for other fine artisans, to make their exhibits more self-supporting.

Ellen and John Blauer pose with some of their highly collectible, finely crafted miniatures.

For those who are new to this business, Mary Lee Tracy cautions about the difficulty of getting into the best shows: "We got in because Tracy had something really good and different. There were lots of little instruments, but none that really worked. We also got in because we were aggressive. Tracy spent about five hundred dollars on phone calls, checking shows around the country and making sure he got a place for himself."

Unlike the Blauers, with their twenty-year-old business, the Tracys are still taking things a step — or rather a show — at a time. They don't want to produce their own shows, but they have talked

When scaled down to miniature proportions, a Chippendale dining room like this steps beyond the definition of reproduction. This was designed and created by Ellen and John Blauer.

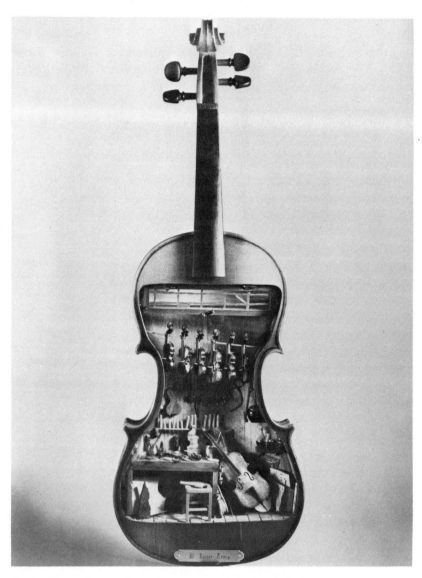

Foster Tracy is a modern-day master of the handmade musical instrument; his tiny gems are exact, playing replicas. Photograph, Kenneth Clare

of opening up a gallery shop for their own and other artisans' miniatures, with an annex for fine-quality supplies.

The range of miniature crafts categories in which the artisan can become involved is virtually endless. Several weavers have found scaled-down traditional coverlets popular collectibles with miniaturists and textile enthusiasts alike. Although these don't command the prices of, say, a miniature Chippendale secretary, they offer the potential for a nice small business for the weaver who enjoys working with fine threads and intricate patterns on projects that go a lot faster than other types of weavings.

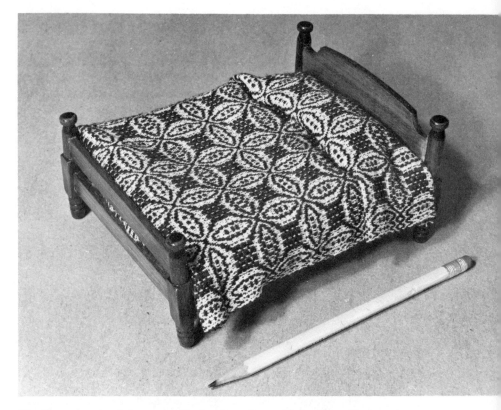

Handwoven coverlets are particular favorites with textile collectors; in miniature they offer the collector something at once old and new.
Photograph, Richard A. Balay; weaver, Charleen Arnold

The coverlets lend themselves to mail order selling very nicely, but Charleen Arnold, of Loveland, Colorado, warns that it is important to have an illustrated price list and sample swatches. If you want your ads to pay off, she suggests that you charge for samples, but make the price applicable to the first order. Taking part in at least local shows is important in creating exposure for your "line," if you want to produce and sell in any kind of volume.

The miniature coverlet can be bought with clearly established provenance; to wit, the weaver at her loom.

CHAPTER 7

❖ ❖ ❖

Writers, Editors, and Publishers

Educators may decry the decline of reading, but if books and newspapers are hard-pressed to compete with television for the public's attention and dollars, the antiques-collectibles hobbyists and professionals are most certainly exceptions. Of the careers thus far discussed, only show promotion is not vitally and constantly concerned with reading for the attainment and maintenance of knowledgeability. Dealers, appraisers, auctioneers, restorers, and conservators, without exception, cite a well-stocked, up-to-date reference library as a "must" investment of time and money. Their needs, along with the hobbyists' and collectors', have quite naturally created yet another career opportunity in the antiques and collectibles field.

Since the late 1960s, an impressive number of newcomers have successfully joined the ranks of the art-antiques-collectibles press. They write a prodigious number of articles, columns, and books. They have also bitten the entrepreneurial bullet to become small, independent publishers, often growing well beyond initial expectations.

Lest all this sound a bit too rosy, we have to note that some publications have been known to go almost as fast as they have come; not every book "takes off" (as a look at the remainder stores will attest), and two-figure article fees are far from uncommon. These caveats notwithstanding, publishing is a facet of the antiques-collectibles business that can be as addictive for some people as collecting is for others. What follows is designed to help you make that addiction pay off.

WRITING CATEGORIES

The types of writing that appear in collectors' periodicals and books can be divided into three basic categories: reportage, how-to or self-help, and historical perspective.

Reportage

Reportage is most common to newspapers and magazines. It includes reports on stores, exhibits, shows, seminars, and auctions — upcoming or reviewed — as well as interviews with people involved in these and other activities. Depending on a publication's staff or the extent of its coverage, this material may be staff-written or bought from free-lance writers. If a free lance does articles of this type for a regular paper, he becomes what is known as a "stringer," meaning that whenever a story is likely to come up in his locale, the editor may assign an article to him. Some larger publications with international coverage, like *Antique Monthly*, put stringers on a steady retainer basis; the writers receive annual retainer fees to do an article per issue, plus others as the need arises.

The key to doing reportage is to provide answers to the questions who, what, where, when, and why, usually called the five basic W's of journalism. Since newspapers frequently cut articles from the end in case of space problems, the W's must be answered at the beginning, with details added in order of importance.

How-To or Self-Help Articles and Books

These include writings that offer help either in identifying and appraising objects or in becoming more effective in a variety of amateur or professional involvements.

Historical Perspective

Historical perspective writing is often combined with how-to and self-help. (This book is a case in point.) An article or book on finding, appraising, and maintaining a type of antique will gain meaning if the writer includes an account and analysis of events and attitudes leading up to the present. Books like *The Elegant Auctioneers* by Wesley Towner and *Art on the Market* by Maurice Rheims (See Part II, Resources) are good examples of perspective books.

THE SOMMER A-B-C WRITING TEST

A rich vocabulary or piquant style is not necessarily crucial for getting into print. Carefully researched facts, couched in clear and simple language, will carry the day with most editors. I can vouch for agents, too, on that score, since I have been an agent for twenty years, not only for my own work but for that of other nonfiction writers. In the latter capacity I have devised what I call the Sommer A-B-C Writing Test, for evaluating the marketability of manuscripts that come in over the transom — a publishing term for unsolicited material.

A: Authenticated information. An article or book about antiques or collectibles without correct detailed information is like a house tottering on a crumbling foundation. Specifically cited reading references, accurately quoted interviews, the author's own experience and background — all are vital to establish the correctness and authenticity of writing.

B: Brevity. I won't go quite so far as Nietzsche when he said, "It is my ambition to say in ten sentences what others have said in a whole book." I would, however, urge all who want to be read to keep in mind that a few well-chosen words may be better than a labored paragraph.

C: Clarity. Editor-publisher Samuel Pennington can take justifiable pride in the fact that his *Maine Antiques Digest,* because of its clear writing, is recommended by English teachers in several states and in the province of Toronto. Writers whose language is unfamiliar to reasonably intelligent readers will reap more censure for pomposity than kudos for cleverness. Clarity also incorporates the writer's understanding of the reader's previous knowledge so that all facts necessary to comprehension are included. In short, don't overdo brevity at clarity's expense!

AUXILIARY SKILLS AND TOOLS

Alert educators have for some time been aware that a solid education should encompass the three R's — reading, 'riting, and 'rithemetic — plus two — typing and photography. What's good for school kids is a practical must for the writer on antiques and collectibles. Whether you type fast or slowly is a matter of your own labor efficiency, but type you must. And because so many articles and books depend on illustrations for authenticity and interest, the ability to take photographs ranks almost as high.

Katharine Morrison McClinton, who has been writing and publishing antiques books since 1929, commented with considerable regret on her one-fingered typing and her inability to take her own photographs. "I don't suppose anyone else would start like me today. For many years I couldn't type at all, and three books really were typed with one finger." The need to depend on professional photographers has been both restrictive and expensive. "If you use museum photos, you have to pay for print plus reproduction fees. If you want a photograph of something in a shop, they usually don't have photos available . . . Only last spring I had to pay someone two hundred dollars for five shots. If you're going to do books, you should be able to take your own pictures." See Photography Know-How, in Part II, Resources.

MARKETING KNOW-HOW

Periodicals

Okay, you've got an idea for an article or a series. How do you go about getting it into print?

The Resources section of this book lists most of the antiques periodicals where your material may find a home. The *Writer's Market* prints details, under the classification Hobbies, about the buying policies of at least some of these magazines. Two other library references, *Ulrich's International Periodicals Directory* and the *Encyclopedia of Associations,* will be of help. The first lists periodicals by classification; the latter may lead you to publications put out by collectors' organizations. Before you submit something to a magazine, be sure to read at least one issue and write to ask for any available writers' guidelines.

If your article is short and you have no published credits, you may just want to plunge in and submit the entire piece. If so, type it double-space on 8½-by-11-inch paper. Send a brief covering letter and enclose a stamped, self-addressed envelope. If the editor decides not to use the article, he's not obliged to return it unless you've sent along your own envelope.

If your article will involve interviewing or any extensive research, you will save time for yourself and the editor by sending him a brief query summarizing your idea, stating your qualifications, the approximate length of the proposed piece, and number of illustrations, if any. This is your pitch to sell yourself and your idea, to obtain a nod to go ahead. If the editor is interested, chances are it will be with an "on spec" proviso, meaning the idea sounds interesting but acceptance hinges on how you implement it.

Some editors don't mind if you submit photocopies to several publications at the same time. This save you a lot of waiting around, especially if your idea is a very timely one. *Writer's Market* or editorial guideline sheets from individual publications will give multiple submission policies.

Local general papers should not be ignored as article markets. If they don't have any antiques coverage now, they may welcome submissions, especially if you have some expertise. Pay is likely to be very low, but you can submit tear sheets of an article in one paper to noncompeting papers throughout the country, and thus sell your idea a number of times. You'd better check this out, obtaining clearance before you sell off your right to do so.

Books

Since even more books than periodicals are published, the tasks of checking to see if anything else has been written on your subject and finding the name of the most likely publisher would seem to be almost impossible. Actually, both are quite simple.

First, do some browsing in stores to study the new books. Then check the library catalogue and shelves — reading and reference — to get an idea of published titles. To round out this browser's view of what's around, check the reference department of the library for these three sources: (1) *Subject Guide to Books in Print*, to get a list of all the titles on, or similar to, your subject. (2) The most recent fall and spring announcement issues of *Publishers Weekly*, the trade magazine of the publishing world, to see what different publishers are bringing out and to get a general feel for the market. Make a list of publishers who seem like good bets for your book. (3) *Literary Market Place*, in which you will find the name of the editor to whom to write about your idea — either nonfiction or special projects. This will also give you statistics about how many books a publisher puts out each year and how long in business. The *Writer's Market*, mentioned above, also has a section on book publishers, with terms usual for beginning authors.

Submission procedures vary. I've known authors who have completed and sold an entire book manuscript, right down to the illustrations. As a rule, whether you work with an agent or submit independently, it is wiser first to prepare a selling proposal and a brief outline, with a sample chapter, to show your style. The proposal is like the article query, a sales letter. It should summarize the book's intent, your particular focus, and explain how the book differs from any competitive titles. The outline is essentially a table of contents, with annotated chapter headings giving some details about the contents. The proposal, alone or accompanied by a table of contents, can be sent as a query to a number of editors at once, though etiquette calls for your alerting them to the fact that you're doing this.

EXPECTATIONS FOR THE BOOK AUTHOR   Suppose someone loves your outline or your finished manuscript? What can you expect as a payment?

Antiques-collectibles books rarely come within reach of the best-seller lists, and publishers' offers tend to be correspondingly small. What you can expect is an advance payment ($1000 is the absolute minimum anyone should consider) against future royalty earnings. With few exceptions, this advance is expected to cover expenses. Try to have at least some of your photography paid through a nondeductible expense account.

Royalties at a percentage of the list, or cover, price vary, with provisions for increments as sales increase. I've heard of some collectors'-book publishers paying as little as 4 to 6 percent on paperbacks. Five percent should be an absolute rock-bottom starting percentage, though 7 percent and up is more in keeping with modern practice. Hard-cover royalties usually begin at 10 percent. Royalties that are figured on the wholesale price of the book leave the author in an unpredictable position and should be avoided. An outright offer, with no share in the earnings, is an equally poor policy.

A writer's own ability to sell books — via the lecture circuit, an antiques business, collectors' groups — can brighten sales and earnings considerably. If you can and want to sell copies of your own book, try to get the highest possible author-discount rate you can.

Books and articles are often closely linked, with articles leading to invitations to do books, and vice versa. If your article is too closely tied in to a book you've done, the editor is likely to treat it as publicity material and not pay you, though the publicity will help the book's sales. At any rate, having returned to the magazine and newspaper editor and publisher's desks, let us view the opportunities from that particular vantage point.

A View from the Editor's Desk

Editorships entailing full-time managerial duties and a weekly paycheck are less than plentiful. They do, however, exist. A recent issue of *Publishers Weekly* carried a classified ad that read: "EDITOR, ANTIQUES publication. Need innovative person with editorial and writing capability to spark new life into existing magazine. Should be good self-manager with good business sense. Ample responsibility; reports to publisher. Must have an interest, if not a love of collectibles and antiques."

A very usual method is to work oneself up by the girl or guy Friday route or as a free lance. The spread in the salary range, according to Albert Christian Revi, editor-director of *The Spinning Wheel,* is considerable — from $8000 to $20,000 a year. The publication's locale and size have a lot to do with the size of the salary. Mr. Revi got his job after fourteen years in the antiques business and publication of a number of books on antique glass. He put in eight years as *Spinning Wheel*'s contributing editor. He cites other necessary skills: "being able to spell, punctuate and compose a proper sentence better than most authors . . . also having a very long memory or sixth sense that enables the editor to recall where he or she read about the subject of an article submitted and thus spot material which has been gleaned from already published sources." He adds, "For this reason we exchange subscriptions with so many of our colleagues, to save ourselves embarrassment." Mr. Revi attributes the dearth of opportunities for his kind of job to the fact that many antiques publications are edited by the owner-publisher. This, of course, raises the following questions: Who are some of these publishers? How did they get started? Could *you* aspire to such a goal?

A View from the Publisher's Desk

Media marketing experts usually look on any new magazine as a high-risk, high-capitalization venture. The Long Island newspaper *Newsday* once estimated that it costs $500,000 and five years of operating at a loss to make a magazine work. Yet the antiques press, though not without its failures, comprises many modestly launched and lovingly nurtured periodicals in the small to moderately large range. The following profiles illustrate four such ventures. The stories are heartening not only as journalistic success stories, but as examples of successfully initiated and maintained individual enterprise in general.

The Antiquarian: Antiques, Art, Entertainment & Museum Magazine of New York   To start, let's look at the youngest and most regional, in terms of market targeting, of the four to be detailed. *The Antiquarian* was launched in 1975 by Marguerite Cantine and Elizabeth Kilpatrick. Their start-up investment was an amazing $131 — plus three years of working from 9:00 A.M. to 1:30 A.M., fifty weeks a year, and a steady infusion of every penny of profit earned. Contrary to what *Newsday* said, the magazine, in spite of its minimal capitalization, never lost money.

"Our income range is survival right now," Marge Cantine explains, quickly adding that she expects this soon to shift from middle- to upper-middle-income range. "We have come of age, and things have begun to jell." This jelling process includes more free time as well as more money. "People are contracting for ads, which cuts down on road time. Other ads are sent by agencies, which cuts down on layout time. It used to take seven days to put together a magazine; now it takes two."

To go back to that $131 beginning, why did Liz and Marge decide to become publishers, and how did they evolve the slant that makes their magazine uniquely their own?

In her pre-*Antiquarian* days, Liz had little connection with either antiques or journalism; one of her longest-held jobs was that of bartender. Marge, a lifelong antiques buff, directed her career energies to other types of journalism, until an auto accident interrupted her climb up the industrial ladder. Liz quit her job and taught Marge to walk again, and eventually it seemed only natural for this friendship to become a business partnership as well.

As the magazine's subtitle indicates, the appeal goes beyond the antiques collector and dealer, which perhaps offsets the limitations of the magazine's being regional. Circulation has been built from an initial 5000 to a current 10,000, slowly and with an independence of attitude in which the publishers take great pride. Although they have given away their share of free copies, they quickly limited this to shows they consider of top quality. Furthermore, they give away only back issues, in fairness to paying subscribers. They're choosy about the type of advertising they accept, too.

"We can afford to be particular because this entire magazine is put together by exactly two people. We write, photograph, edit, lay out, paste up, mail . . . everything. Every letter is answered personally. Every magazine is quality-controlled." They do use an outside firm for typesetting and pay for printing from camera-ready copy, and they also use some reprint editorial material. The *Antiquarian*'s editors plan to maintain the present intimacy and control over their magazine, but even this controlled growth can accommodate the additional 10,000 subscribers they expect to gain through broadened newsstand distribution. This last is vital to a magazine's health, and Marge issues a word of caution about anyone taking it for granted: "It's a tough market. You have to be seen by a major distributor, judged, and accepted. It took us two years to crack Citywide [a major distributor] stands and another two months to crack Eastern." In spite of the market's being a tough one, Marge and Liz consider it wide open, if you can sell yourself. This poem, written by Marge Cantine when she was twenty-two, sums up their experiences to date.

> I would have proved to be
> A much more reckless woman
> Than I am
> Had I never gambled once
> Losing the chance to win.

The Maine Antiques Digest: The Marketplace for Americana   In response to a question about her own reading-list musts, Marguerite Cantine gave *Maine Antiques Digest* top priority. "I love it. I don't know Sam and he doesn't know me, but I love the hell out of him. He's got it all together." No small compliment this, coming from someone as painstakingly honest as Marge!

There are times when at least some of the *Digest*'s 13,000 readers don't quite share Marge's love for this monthly tabloid's outspoken editor-publisher, Samuel Pennington. However, even those who disapprove of some of the things he says and does, respect his thorough, lucid reporting and enjoy the many photos, which carry prices in the captions.

The *Digest* is just a year older than *The Antiquarian*. It began with even less journalistic know-how (Pennington is a retired air force major) and on an only relatively longer shoestring — $2500. Sam and his co-editor wife, Sally, did know the antiques business both as collectors and, for a while, as dealers. By utilizing every available informational resource, such as the printing experts at the Maine *Times* and publishing trade journals like *Folio* (P.O. Box 697, New

Canaan, Connecticut 06840), the rest of the Penningtons' education as editors and publishers developed.

The decision to specialize in regional Americana but to slant news to a national readership with an established interest and knowledge gave the paper an immediate and lasting image and acceptance. Distributing nationally and costing space ads for easy affordability helped to extend the advertising base beyond the Maine borders. Although the *Digest* is teeming with ads, this phase of the business gives some cause for concern. In response to my question as to whether Sam thought too many antiques publications might be spoiling the broth, he said, "I think readers will take everything that's good, but the advertising can get to be a very competitive problem."

Sam and Sally Pennington continue as editor and co-editor, as they have since the *Digest*'s birth. The fact that they have been able to create jobs for half a dozen others besides themselves adds considerably to their pride and pleasure in the paper. This enlarged staff seems to pose no threat to the personal quality and content control. Sam Pennington, camera and lights always at hand, continues to be a strongly felt presence wherever the news scent leads — be it to a local auction or a seminar held in New York by a publishing colleague, Gray Boone.

Antique Monthly: The Nation's Finest Antiques Newspaper   With a circulation of 100,000 and still going strong, *Antique Monthly* has caught up nicely with two of the oldest and most successful publications in the field, the magazine *Antiques* and *The Antiques Trader Weekly*. (The latter does remain in the forefront when its weekly 90,000 circulation is counted up on a monthly basis.) The *Antique Monthly*'s climb into the big league is noteworthy because, like *The Antiquarian* and *The Maine Antiques Digest*, it started very small and continues to operate in a manner that, though considerably grander in scale, would make many a New York publisher sigh with envy and admiration.

Gray Boone describes her beginning in publishing as that of just another example of a housewife who turned her hobby into a business, right from the kitchen table. True enough, but this must be tempered with the explanation that Mrs. Boone has never been "just a housewife" in the usual sense of that phrase. Like many Southern

*Wherever there is news to cover and questions to ask for his readers —
be it in Maine or a New York hotel ballroom — editor-publisher Sam
Pennington is sure to be on the spot.*

women, she embodies that unbeatable combination of feminine charm and good looks with keen intelligence and a strong self-image and sense of purpose. She studied international law in college and is married to a newspaper publisher. She did pay for the use of her husband's plant facilities from the start, but the connection was an obvious advantage. Since the paper's early days, the Boones have moved their business from Norfolk, Virginia, to Tuscaloosa, Alabama, where they share a building to house their combined presses.

Aside from the foregoing modifications of the simple housewife success story, the Boone paper *was* born out of an avocational enthusiasm for antiques and without far-reaching growth plans or financial investment. From 1967 until just before 1969, the *Monthly* was, in fact, a quarterly, and Gray did everything herself — from copy, advertising, and printing (learned from her husband's staff), to distribution. She printed 5000 copies of the first eight-page issue only because she had an auctioneer friend who said she could use his mailing list. Three thousand copies were thus mailed out as "freebies," and the rest were taken in the car and dumped, twenty-five at a time, with antiques dealers, who were asked to pass them along to customers.

As we have seen, the growth of a publication is very much determined by the focus of the editorial approach. Gray Boone's coverage of everything within the cover of "fine antiques" set the stage for her reaching a large nationwide readership. Of course, wanting to reach a particular audience and doing so are different matters. In Gray's case, the result is attributable to a combination of good fortune and exceptionally effective management of time and money.

Good fortune came in the way of a birthday gift from her father-in-law — an ad for her venture in a very large magazine, *Southern Living*. The response to the ad turned the tide for the paper's advertising strength and moved it into the monthly category, with a staff of three.

The Boone time-and-management methods center on the telephone. "I perfected doing not only advertising and circulation business by phone, but interviewing and building up a list of roving editors and stringers," she told me. "I *live* with the phone, and that includes conference calls and transatlantic calls." She conceded that her phone bills are staggering, "but it's a lot less time and money than setting up offices in different places. It makes absolutely no difference where I live."

The annual Antique Monthly Conference in New York was conceived as a prestige-building and educational project to bring to-

Most times, Gray Boone conducts her newspaper business by burning up the telephone wires between Tuscaloosa, Alabama, and the rest of the world. Once a year, she brings the antiques world together for the Antique Monthly Conference. She moderates the discussions with unruffled enjoyment.

gether collectors, dealers, and museum people from all over the world. It's not a moneymaker like the paper, but it does pay for itself and, more important, has led to yet another type of publishing — a weekly newsletter, *The Gray Letter*.

Newsletter publishing has not reached anywhere near the proportion of the general antiques press; yet there have been enough entrants into the field to give rise to speculation that the end is indeed not in sight. One of the most unusual, least likely to lend itself to copying, takes us to our final profile in this section.

The Monthly Art Sales Index   Unlike the newspaper and magazine publisher who mainly relies on advertising revenues for his profit, the newsletter publisher earns his income from subscribers who will pay higher than usual rates if the newsletter delivers intensely concentrated, exclusive information faster and more conveniently than other sources.

Richard Hislop, an Englishman with a background in business machine sales (including computers) and a fondness for fine paintings, has managed to consolidate these two seemingly disparate interests into a prosperous publishing business. What he has done is to harness the computer to the task of recording some 35,000 worldwide auction sales results of about 10,000 different artists. Ten newsletters a year are issued. To enlarge the market for his information, as well as the profits, he issues *The Annual Art Sales Index,* a bound volume. Still another publication, a quarterly giving art market trends (*Art Investment Guide*) is not so profitable, but it is a public relations response to reader requests.

As different as all this sounds from the Cantine and Kilpatrick, Pennington, and Gray ventures, it, too, is a case history of individual enterprise. Richard Hislop did it all himself, without major investment in either equipment or staff and office space. He leases a computer once a month, has one agent in Paris, and if he can't get to a sale himself or needs quick information, he will pay someone to attend a sale on a free-lance basis. The *Art Index* office is the Hislop home, and the staff consists of his wife and a few free lances, who come in to suit their particular private schedules.

Perhaps if the *Index* had been more generously capitalized at the outset, it would not have taken five years or been quite as much of a struggle. Mr. Hislop confides, "At the beginning I had to limit traveling for lack of money — and now I have to limit it for lack of time." His pride and enthusiasm for the present and future achievements of his computerized information terminal bubbles forth from beneath his English composure. "I am mining a thin stream of gold. When the time comes for people to use their own computer terminals I could set up to plug in within six months." Even now he has worked out an individualized service whereby people can obtain very specific types of artist information from his data bank. Asked about potential competition, he said he felt his five-year headstart would be hard to match. This may be discouraging for anyone else, but then who's to say there isn't a reader out there who can't do for something else, or in some other innovative way, what Richard Hislop has done for painting?

The Self-Publishing Route

Before we leave the subject of publishing opportunities, I'd like to discuss one more way of enjoying the challenges and rewards of being the captain of one's own publication efforts, without the pressures of deadlines — namely, self-publishing. This means that once you come up with an idea for a book, you by-pass the process of selling a publisher on its worth. Instead, you write, produce, and distribute it all yourself. If doing it all alone seems overwhelming, there is plenty of help available in the form of free-lance editors and artists, printers, and distributors. One word of warning: Do not confuse self-publishing with vanity or subsidy publishing. Under such an arrangement — and it's usually expensive — you pay someone else to take on your book, and you have no control of the management and earnings.

Directories

Directories are a favorite type of self-publishing venture because they present the option of including ads, which will pay for at least part of the expenses, and they can be updated regularly, thus providing a nice continuing project.

A somewhat spectacular directory success is the *Lyle Official Antiques Review*. This distinguished-looking, widely advertised and distributed annual began quite humbly as a price list. The *Review's* publisher is a former London picker named Tony Curtis. When dealers asked him repeatedly for copies of the typed lists with little sketches he used to leave behind to show what he wanted, he decided to sell the list. A small newspaper ad offering the list brought over 600 responses, and since then Curtis has gone from small self-publisher to head of a publishing empire, appropriately housed in a Scottish mansion. Some 45,000 copies of the *Review* are printed, along with numerous other titles. "Lyle" is a made-up name that Curtis felt would give class to his reviews, and the word "Official," according to an article in the *New York Times*, was added on the advice of an American friend, who told Curtis the extra word was "harmless" and would double sales.

Directories need not be fat and sassy like the *Lyle Review*. To illustrate this and at the same time point out the option of moving back and forth between conventional publishing and self-publishing, I cite one of my own ventures into these waters, a pamphlet-sized publication called *The Annotated Directory of Self-Published Textile Books*. Through my own involvement in the textile arts, both past and present, and in the course of writing a commercially published book on textile collecting (*Textile Collector's Guide*), I became familiar with a wide variety of books, published by the authors, in this particular area. I felt these would make interesting and informative collectibles themselves for textile artists, for collectors of textiles, and collectors of limited-edition, small-press efforts. The potential audience was easily reachable and called for a small printing, which makes the booklet itself eligible as a collectible. To add a note of provenance and at the same time give other interested self-publishers some information on the basic decision-making, editorial, and distribution process, I produced a two-page insert called *The Making of the Annotated Directory of Self-Published Textile Books*. (See Part II, Resources, for how to obtain.)

To conclude this discussion, let's consider a very different kind of informational book. Its publisher is Hope Peek, who, together with Jackie Oosthuizen, runs Constantia Antiques, specializing in fine small objects. Hope also loves to cook, and on coming across that book rarity, an eighteenth-century cookbook, got the idea of adapting some of the recipes for the modern cook. "The idea teased me

ANNOTATED

DIRECTORY OF SELF-PUBLISHED

TEXTILE BOOKS

Elyse Sommer, Editor
Copyright 1977
ISBN No. 0-9601498-1-3
Library of Congress Catalogue
 Card No. 77-91816
First Edition, 2000 copies

No compensation has been received
for inclusion of any books listed.
Omissions are due to the problems
inherent in all self-publication,
namely, the difficulties of publici-
zing one's existence!

CONTENTS

Please send recommendations for inclusion in future editions, orders
for extra copies of this edition, inquiries about other books, and lectures about textile collecting or self-publishing to:

Sommertime Publications
P.O. Box E
Woodmere, L.I., N.Y. 11598

Title page of limited edition directory for special-interest collectors.

constantly until I produced a manuscript. I also decided, while turn-ing out the text, to publish it myself . . . and to follow that item with a series of related volumes over the next several years." The fifty-four-page booklet that resulted from this idea is a small gem, both in contents and appearance. With the help of her husband's expertise in the area of graphics and promotion, Hope Peek created outstand-ing art work for the book and its attendant promotional literature.

Antique Desserts had a first printing of 10,000 copies, which is rather large for a small-press effort and takes this out of the limited-edition (2000 copies or less), rare-books range. Nevertheless, there are some collectors who seek selected nonlimited editions by private publishers. Whether the book becomes a collectible or not, it is well on the way to a satisfactory sale. Several leading magazines have given it editorial coverage, and some of the best museum shops are happy to distribute this fine effort.

Hope Peek's cookbook, which she published herself, blends perfectly with some of the objects sold through her business, Constantia Antiques.

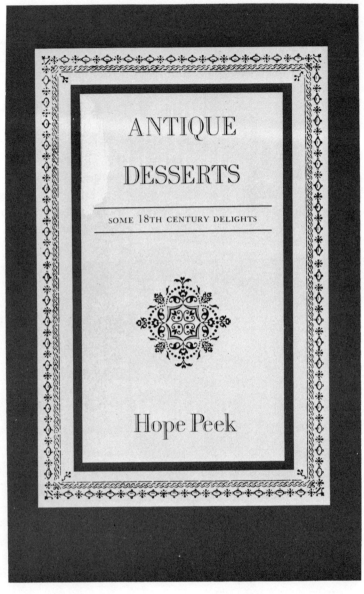

This close-up view of the cover shows how well the design echoes the feeling of fine china.

CHAPTER 8

❖ ❖ ❖

Spinoffs

The average merchant finds the key to financial success in steady, repeat sales made through reliable channels of merchandise supply. The difficulties of inventory replacement peculiar to the antiques-collectibles trade account for an increasing interest in careers not dependent on the vagaries of the marketplace, since income then derives from fees paid for knowledge or service. Most of these activities have already been fully described. Following are some elaborations and variations for capitalizing on antiques-collectibles–related interests, skills, and know-how, as well as for creating and finding sources for compatible or tie-in products.

LECTURING

Lecture opportunities run the gamut from talks to small groups at libraries and clubs to huge crowds gathered in college auditoriums and hotel ballrooms. Depending on the audience and the sponsors, lectures may cover such topics as Collecting for Fun and Profit, Trash or Treasures, Corporate Collecting, The Tax Law and the Collector and Dealer, Detecting Fakes, The History of Pressed Glass, and so forth. Fees may range from quid pro quo lecture-for-publicity arrangements to small honorariums to good-sized fees. Although antiques lecturers are a far cry from the big-time celebrity speakers who draw five-figure fees, the antiques world does have its own stars. For example, Robert Bishop, the director of the American Museum of Folk Art, is considered an outstanding drawing card, not only because of his impressive credentials and achievements (dealer, author, teacher, museum administrator), but because of his personal magnetism and effectiveness as a speaker.

Lack of a national reputation or prestigious degrees and connections will not preclude your becoming a sought-after lecturer — provided you have something worthwhile to say and know how to convey it to an audience. Joan and Raymond Chambers, for example, are known mainly in New York and Long Island, where they do some 125 slide lectures a year under the sponsorship of the New York Telephone Company. The lectures evolved from their very extensive collection of Long Island newspapers, maps, books, and other historical material.

Mr. Chambers started it all by talking informally about his collection before groups of friends. He then got the idea of a more professional show business–type of presentation, which led to more professional, paid engagements. With the help of Joan's research and illustrative art work, one lecture led to another until the couple built up a repertoire of nineteen. When a representative from the telephone company, who had seen the Chamberses in action, suggested hiring them on a retainer basis, to give talks the company would arrange and pay for, they agreed. It meant that groups without lecture budgets could book the programs, and it also eliminated a lot of record-keeping.

Corporate sponsors ready to underwrite the cost and to promote a set of lectures are few and far between, even for those with the versatility to put together a lot of different programs. However, since you never can tell who's going to be in the audience, even your $25 talk for a local library or church should be your best lecture. Further-

Here we see one of the "stars" of the antiques lecture circuit, Dr. Robert Bishop, of the American Museum of Folk Art.

more, take heed of this bit of advice from Ben Franklin: "He that waits upon fortune is never sure of dinner." Let people know what you can do and keep letting them know, following these basic guidelines:

1. Try to dream up a title that will capture the essence of your lecture. Summarize the salient features of your presentation, including any visual accompaniments. State the approximate length and any possible follow-up lectures. Type all this on an 8½-by-11-inch sheet of paper, including your name, address, and telephone number. Send copies, with a brief covering letter, to various groups. (Check the *Encyclopedia of Associations*, Part II, Resources, for national groups.) You can tack some of the sheets to bulletin boards of stores or tape them to store windows.

2. Using your lecture title as the lead-in and cutting the descriptive information to the bare bones, run some ads in your local giveaway paper.

3. Once you get your first lecture appointment, be sure to check out the physical arrangements, the scheduled time, and how to get to the hall or library. Rehearse and rehearse again. A really well-prepared lecture pays off.

4. During those nervous first minutes of the lecture, make eye contact with a friendly sympathetic face. Remember, everyone is tense at first. It passes. Concentrate on your subject. Be authoritative, but avoid the *I* emphasis.

5. Prepare some handout, giveaway material — a list of books for further reference, a list of recommended exhibits or museums, six to ten checkpoints from the lecture. People like to come away with something concrete, a reminder of an event. If you put on the handout your name and address and telephone number and the title of the lecture you gave (plus others you are prepared to give), the small offset expenditure is sure to lead to future invitations.

6. Save any newspaper write-ups of your lecture as well as complimentary personal notes. When you get enough of these together, you can have them offset and send them out with any lecture solicitations.

HOBBIES AND SKILLS

8400-0 Flea Markets! Town and Country
9 sessions. Sat., 12 noon-3:00 pm, beg. Mar. 18. $80.
MARJORIE FRIEDMAN, SUE BERKMAN, CARA GREENBERG
Springtime is the flea-"bug" season. Once bitten—browsers, collectors and dealers scour the country-side for *strikes* and *finds*. Join the fun. Eight Saturdays to learn and buy—antiques, collectibles, and bargains. One week-end to make the scene: showing, selling and dealing.

Mar. 18 Meeting at The New School: Markets in general, the New York scene, in particular; sources of local and tri-state information, buying guides. Finding a specialty among the range of antique wares.

Apr. 1 Soho/Canal: "rags" in Canal Street Flea Markets to riches in the Soho Antique shops.

Apr. 8 Englishtown, New Jersey: The archetype of flea markets, acres of bargains for early risers. Learn this subculture's manners and mores.

Apr. 15 Meeting at The New School: Buying for resale—for those who might want to sell, reappraisal of the "Junque" in the garage. What's moving, fix-it places, foretelling trends, buying for investment.

Apr. 22 The New Hope scene: From Lambertville, New Jersey to Lahaska, Pa. Five flea markets for browsing and buying.

Apr. 29 Meeting at the New School: Treasures and Traps. Legalities, licensing, turning a hobby into a business.

May 6 "Village" shopping in the city. Bleecker Street and Hudson setting the tone for antique/flea collections.

May 13 Promotion and planning. A guest promoter tells how to prepare an outdoor exhibit. Renting space, security, salesmanship, mark-up, paid advertising, record keeping inventories. Scheduling show-time responsibilities.

May 20 Show-time. Exhibitors share the cost of renting space; others select their own role—as watchers, helpers and browsers. (The show-place to be determined.)

Note: This schedule subject to alternate plans and modifications to allow time for new shows and exhibits.

The teacher of an adult education or college extension course needs to prepare an outline that will induce the program director to offer the course — and the potential student to register.

TEACHING

Formal college curriculums in the antiques business as a profession seem more than a speculative eventuality. In the meantime, continuing education programs throughout the country are most hospitable to proposals for courses in the antiques area. In addition to providing steady pay, at least for the run of the course, teaching builds a continuing and stimulating interrelationship that is not attainable from lecturing on a one-time basis.

If you wish to explore teaching possibilities, round up the course offerings from schools, recreational centers, and college extension programs within accessible range. Study the course descriptions to get the feel for the overall program and your possible place within it. Writing up a course proposal is very much like submitting a book outline. Instead of listing your table of contents with annotations about what each chapter will cover, write a one-liner for each session, with fill-in descriptions. Address a brief covering letter to the person in charge, explaining why you would like to offer the course and listing your credentials. If your course is accepted, this proposal will probably be the copy for the brochure, so give it your maximum effort; it has to attract both the program planner and, more important, the potential student. No enrollment, no course!

Unless a course is organized to fill numerous and specific requests, it's always something of a horse race. The New School in New York City, the oldest and biggest adult school in the country, issues a catalogue of 200 enticing pages or more twice a year. Yet, in spite of the pizazz of the catalogue and the copy, as many as half of the course offerings never get off the ground for lack of minimum enrollment.

One teacher whose course did make it is Marjorie Friedman. Her idea for a flea market course grew out of her own part-time experience as a city and country flea market dealer. An English teacher who had fallen victim to the City University's financial squeeze in the midst of completing her Ph.D. thesis, she found in the flea market world relief from Academe's pressures, along with about $300 a weekend ("We worked on low markup and high turnover!"). She thought her New School course proposal would squeeze through with the required enrollment of ten students. Instead, sixty people signed up for the first semester, eighty for the second. Marjorie was a New School star. To help her cope with the large classes, she enlisted two other antiquers, Sue Berkman and Cara Greenberg, as coteachers.

Aware of the transience of extension school stardom, Marjorie has designed a number of other courses on a somewhat more scholarly level. These must meet the test of an increased number of excellent offerings by other schools in and around town, such as Hunter College's Lifelong Learning Center's courses, taught by experts from the auction world. Thus, though a big city may offer many more teaching opportunities, those of you in quieter areas need not despair. Your course, if accepted, is likely to run longer than in the big city's show business orientation.

LEGAL AID

Burt Fendelman has tied his intense interest in folk art, particularly painted furniture, into his career as a corporate lawyer. He and his wife, Helaine, have collected in more than dilettante fashion. They have done some dealing, mostly to trade up, researched their field carefully, and become personally acquainted with many of the leading folk art collectors and professionals. Most of their friends are collectors and dealers, and it is thus not surprising that when any of them encounter legal problems connected with taxes, insurance, or collections, they call on Burt as their attorney. His familiarity with the field and sympathetic understanding of their particular problems make his services far more valuable than those of another lawyer.

Helaine, who retired from teaching to raise two youngsters, has applied the research and communication training of her first career to her own collector-related spinoff activities. She researched a special area of folk art in need of a book, tramp art. This proved unrewarding financially, but it did ensure her a secure place in the hierarchy of folk art experts, and led to an invitation for her and Burt to be guest curators of an exhibition at the American Museum of Folk Art. This, like her additional work for the museum's Friends Committee, was volunteer work, but it gave her the experience that warranted her asking for, and getting, a paid position as advertising manager of the museum's quarterly, *The Clarion*. As collector and dealer friends trust Burt Fendelman as their lawyer, so advertisers trust and respect and *buy* space from Helaine. The Fendelmans eventually would like to become fine-furniture dealers, but for the present their multiple spinoff involvements are keeping them happily busy.

ADVERTISING AND PROMOTION

During the course of gathering information for this book, I noticed a number of ads for space sales jobs in other publications. Spinoff opportunities like Helaine Fendelman's job, then, are not limited to New York. Many dealers, auctioneers, promoters, large shippers, and importers use the services of professionals for advertising or promotion or both. A knowledge of antiques is not a prerequisite for creating good copy or layout or for planning an effective promotional campaign; on the other hand, it won't hurt. Several ad and promotion agencies have become known as antiques specialists.

CORPORATE HISTORIANS AND PROMOTERS

Many forward-looking companies have become aware of the public relations value of preserving their past records and products. Much of the Libbey-Owens-Ford Glass Company's history has been brought into full focus through the in-depth scholarship of a longtime employee, Carl Fauster, and this scholarship has, in turn, brought its own rewards and pleasures to Mr. Fauster. While working for Libbey-Owens-Ford, first as a salesman and later as advertising and merchandise manager, Mr. Fauster's prime concerns were with current production, but requests for help from various writers served to trigger a growing interest in glass history and collecting. His hobby began to assume vocational proportions, and eventually he opted for early retirement in order to become a dealer, writer, and historian in the field of historic glass. One of his endeavors, a reprint

After many years of being involved with contemporary Libbey-Owens Glass sales, Carl Fauster has become a full-time collector-dealer-writer-publisher-lecturer in the area of antique glass.

of an 1896 Libbey catalogue, has been bought by collectors, dealers, and historians. He is cofounder of the Glass Collectors Club of Toledo and founder of the Antique & Historic Glass Foundation Project. He lectures, writes, and publishes.

For companies without a Carl Fauster, or with products less readily discernible in terms of collectible value, two Philadelphians have set up a consultation service they call Corporate Collectibles.

Dr. Howard Applegate is a former academic; Will Roberts is a public relations expert. Together, they share a long-standing interest in such collectibles as automotive literature and commercial containers. They feel many companies are simply not aware of the collecting interest in the things they throw out. Their aim is to alert such companies to the public relations and sales impact of the vast and increasingly diversified collecting population and to help them maintain archival and informational services. They use their skills and know-how about collectibles to design and produce company catalogues or value guides. Dr. Applegate especially has a knack for spotting collecting potential in the most obscure and unlikely objects, so companies using their services are likely to be in for some surprises. When these two gentlemen came to my home for an interview, Dr. Applegate disappeared into the kitchen long enough to retrieve two embarrassingly old containers from the spice cabinet. Their out-of-use labels, minus the currently dominant Universal Product Code stamp, apparently more than offset my untidy housekeeping. He bore away my "gift" with the pride of a high bidder at a Sotheby Parke Bernet auction.

ANTIQUE PHOTOGRAPHY

The burgeoning interest in photographica has spurred many dealerships, as already illustrated in Chapter 4. Some who become interested in antique cameras and their products are craftsmen who like to restore the old cameras. Others are photographers interested in reviving old photographic techniques.

Photographer Doug Elbinger turned his fascination with the tintype cameras used by old-time itinerant portraitists into a thriving service business. He used an actual tintype to study and learn the old method and then reproduced an exact replica — but with a dry plate, which does not require the dangerous chemicals used in the originals. With his new equipment and a variety of old costumes, he became a modern-day itinerant photographer at antiques shows and crafts fairs. He became so successful that he was able to set up a permanent studio.

As the tintype business grew, Doug decided to produce his camera and plates in quantity and to sell the equipment, along with information for setting up a similar business. This has become so popular that imitators followed. Anyone interested in this type of business can compare the offerings of Elbinger & Son, Incorporated (2345 Hamilton Road, Okemos, Michigan 48865) with those of others who advertise their wares and services in camera magazines.

ART WORK WITH AN ANTIQUE THEME

As the antiques business grows and people in it become more aware of the value of attractive posters, stationery, business cards, the artist with a fondness for the antique subject may find more and more opportunities to sell sketches and designs. When Helen Grey retired to a very small California desert community, she developed the idea of a mail order business that would offer custom stationery

Small living quarters prevents Artist Helen Grey from collecting antiques. Instead, she designs stationery geared to antiques subjects.

designs especially for antiques collectors and dealers. Through ads in magazines like *Hobbies* and word-of-mouth recommendations, she has built up an enjoyable, unpressured business that leaves her a comfortable profit. Her best customers have been doll and clock collectors and clubs, and she has designed a line of stationery that requires only an imprint to be personalized or can be used "as is." She creates her customized designs after corresponding with clients about their particular interests. For Mrs. Kathleen Crispin, Helen's designs helped to identify Davileen Antiques as specialists in lamps and pottery.

DISTRIBUTING COMPATIBLE PRODUCTS

What represents an original creative effort for Helen Grey or Hope Peek can be a source of extra profits for a dealer. Small book publishers are eager to have retailers who are willing to carry their books, and, though a dealer's percentage on a $3.95 book doesn't amount to much, a dozen or more sales add up nicely. And, of course, reorders present no problem at all. (Constantia Books, Box 1137, Greenwich, Connecticut 06830). Helen Grey's gift packages of notepapers, without imprints, are available on a wholesale basis as gift items. (12505 Royal Road, Space 36, El Cajon, California 92021). In Chapter 3, Mel Nash was seen earning extra income from consigned needlework pillows and a seasoned salt discovered during a trip to New Orleans and now bought from its manufacturer by the caseload.

Some products can be sold under your own company label. For example, Sheila Goldman and Don Salzman (see Chapter 5) have paid lots of bills with a spray to refinish leather on antique cars. This was bought cheaply from the manufacturer and repackaged.

Compatible merchandise is by no means restricted to small-ticket items. Gift and merchandise centers like the one at 225 Fifth Avenue in New York, and nationally scheduled gift shows throughout the country (for schedules, write to Little Management, 261 Madison Avenue, New York, New York 10016), are sources for imported and domestic-reproduction items. These include copper and brass and rugs, which, if not mixed in with or misrepresented as antiques, can enhance stock — and stock turnover.

PART II

❖ ❖ ❖

Resources

CHAPTER 9

❖ ❖ ❖

In-Print
Information

Listings of particular publications and organizations should not be
interpreted as an unqualified endorsement by the author. Your own
ends must determine your needs.

THE ART-ANTIQUES-COLLECTIBLES PRESS

The following list concentrates on American publications devoted
to art-antiques-collectibles interests, as well as on some published in
Canada and Great Britain. Unless otherwise indicated, the scope is
national. General and business publications with regular art and
antiques coverage — such as Rita Reif's columns for the *New York
Times* and Bradley Hitchings' column, Personal Business, for *Business
Week* — are not included.

For special-interest and organization-sponsored publications,
readers are referred to *Ulrich's International Periodicals Directory* and
the *Encyclopedia of Associations;* for additional international publications, to *Ulrich's* or *The International Antiques Yearbook* (see Primary
Reference Directories).

Circulation figures are included wherever available, obtained either directly from publishers or from the *Ayer Directory of Publications* or *Ulrich's*. Annotations about advertising and free-lance opportunities are for purposes of overall perspective. Interested readers are advised to request advertising and writing guidelines from individual publishers.

Americana, American Heritage Publishing Co., 10 Rockefeller Plaza, New York, NY 10020. Bimonthly. Cir., 200,000. $12 a year; single issue, $2.50. Editor, Michael Durham.

Glossy magazine offering a mixture of service articles on old recipes, crafts, and collecting. Uses free-lance articles at rates of about 10 percent of the cost of full-page ads, which range from about $500 for black and white to $3300 for color.

American Antiques, New Hope, PA 18939. Monthly. Cir., 30,000. $10 a year; single issue, $1. Editor, William M. Rivinus.

Smooth-paper magazine covering fine antiques, with emphasis on Americana. Free-lance articles, "coming events," announcements of shows and educational events, classified section. Full-page ad, $300.

American Art and Antiques, Billboard Publications, 1515 Broadway, New York, NY 10036. Bimonthly. $18 a year; single issue, $2.50. Editor, Susan Meyer.

A 1978 entry into the ranks of plush antiques consumer magazines, by the publishers of *American Artist* magazine. Hard-cover binding, lots of color, authoritative free-lance articles.

American Art Journal, 40 W. 57 St., New York, NY 10019. Monthly. $12 a year; $21, two years.

Subtitled "The Serious Magazine on American Art History," this is copublished by two of the biggest names in American art and antiques: Kennedy Galleries and Israel Sack, Inc. No-advertising policy adds to its prestige for contributing authors.

American Collector, 13920 Mt. McClellan Blvd., Reno, NV 89506. Monthly tabloid. Cir., 50,000. $8 a year; $14, two years; $20, three years. Editor, John Maloney.

Editorial emphasis on collectibles, from photo albums to Elvis Presley memorabilia. Some free-lance pieces. Large classified section.

American Collector's Journal, P.O. Box 1431, Porterville, CA 93257. Monthly tabloid. $5 a year; $9, two years; $9.05, three years; single issue, 50¢. Publisher, Leonard Sime.
    Antiques, nostalgia, collectibles, hobbies. Mostly classifieds.

Antiquarian, 13 Cheshire St., Huntington Station, NY 11746. Monthly. Cir., 10,000. $7.50 a year; single issue, 75¢. Editors, Marguerite Cantine, Elizabeth Kilpatrick.
    Focus, New York; slant, entertainment. Staff-written. See Chapter 7.

Antique & Collectors' Mart, P.O. Box 17063, Wichita, KS 67217. Monthly tabloid. $5.50 a year; $10, two years.
    Two-year-young paper aimed at bringing antiques-collectibles information to Midwest. Good market-trends column by Jack Lawton Webb.

Antique Collecting, Box 327, Ephrata, PA 17522. Monthly. Cir., almost 20,000. $10 a year; $18, two years. Editor, Peter Colby.
    Glossy magazine with color. Free-lance articles, with emphasis on author's authority.

Antique Gazette, 929 Davidson Dr., Nashville, TN 37205. Monthly tabloid. $5 a year; $9.50, two years; single issue, 50¢. Editor, Peggy B. Turner.
    Focuses on South, with few by-lined features.

Antique Monthly, P.O. Drawer 2, Tuscaloosa, AL 35401. Monthly tabloid. Cir., 100,000. $9.50 a year; single issue, $1. Editor, Gray D. Boone.
    Flourishing paper, bulging with articles and ads. According to advertising brochure, one-half of national readership in the $20,000 and up annual income range; one-third own stocks and investments above $10,000; and one-quarter have done postgraduate work. Full

page ad costs $756. Has classified section, but display probably what counts here. See Chapter 7.

Antique Trader Weekly, Babka Publishing Co., Inc., Box 1050, Dubuque, IA 52001. Weekly tabloid. Cir., 90,000. $7, six months; $12, one year. Editor, Kyle D. Husfloen.

The *Trader,* as most call it, is a combination of must reading and addiction for people in all walks of antiques. Even full-page ads are basically classifieds, and enough of them appear consistently to indicate that they do well for the advertisers. Some articles and columns.

Antiques and Auction News (Joel Slater's), Box 225, W. Market St., Marietta, PA 17547. Biweekly tabloid. $6 a year. Editor, Joel Slater.

Advertisers of this newspaper will reach 10,000 subscribers and a possible 50,000 others, since that many extra are printed as giveaways at shows. Collectibles interests. Lots of show announcements.

Antiques and The Arts Weekly, Bee Publishing Co., Newtown, CT 06470. Weekly tabloid. Cir., 30,000. $8, one year; $15, two years. Editor, R. Scudder Smith.

A favorite with pros in New York, New Jersey, Connecticut, and other New England states. Focus on staff news. Lots of ads, which can be placed separately from Newtown *Bee,* of which it is a part.

Antiques Dealer, Ebel-Doctorow Publishers, Inc., 1115 Clifton Ave., Clifton, NJ 07013. Monthly. Cir., 8000. $12 a year; single issue, $2. Editor, Stella Hall.

Slim, smooth-paper magazine focusing strictly on people in the antiques business, with subscriptions limited to those submitting letterheads or business cards as proof of professional involvement. Free-lance articles bought at $1 an inch, or $30 a page. Full-page ads, $340.

Antiques Journal, Babka Publishing Co., Inc., Box 1046, Dubuque, IA 52001. Monthly. Cir., 32,699. $7.95 a year; $12.95, two years; $21.95, three years; single issue, $1. Editor, John Mebane.

Magazine arm of *The Antique Trader Weekly*. Free-lance articles on antiques and collectibles ($30 to $105). Lots of book and service-product ads. Classified section.

Antiques Observer, Panax of Virginia, Inc., 3847 Pickett Rd., Fairfax, VA 22030. Monthly tabloid. $6 a year; $10, two years; 60¢, single issue. Editor, Vincent E. Dean.

Targeted toward states of New York, Pennsylvania, Maryland, Virginia, North Carolina, and South Carolina. Antiques-collectibles news and ads.

Antiques Trade Gazette, Metropress Ltd., 116 Long Acre, London WC2 9PA, England. Weekly tabloid. $40 a year, air mail. Editor, Ivor Turnbull.

International auction news, market surveys, and other trade news. Classified ads include situations vacant and wanted.

Antiques World, 122 E. 42 St., New York, NY 10017. Monthly. $18 a year; $2.50, single issue. Editor, Lisa Hammel.

Glossy magazine launched under auspices of *Art News*. Initial November 1978 issue aimed at a projected 40,000 subscribers, ranging from beginning to advanced collectors and including dealers and curators. Focus, international, with emphasis on good writing. Free-lance rates on par with other smooth-paper magazines, though not the very big general-interest ones. Ads available in black and white, two and four color, from business-card size ($215) to full page ($1100–$1395).

Apollo Magazine, 22 Davies St., London. New York subscription office, 75 Rockefeller Plaza, New York, NY 10019. Monthly. $48 a year; $5, single issue. Editor, Denys Sutton.

International prestige magazine of the arts.

Art-Antiques Investment Report, Wall Street Reports, 1230 Wall St., New York, NY 10005. Biweekly newsletter. $125 a year. Editor-publisher, Richard A. Holman.

Three-page newsletter recommended by a number of upper-echelon professionals for good international art market coverage. Condensed version appears as a column, Connoisseur's Corner, in a fat weekly investment newspaper, *The Wall Street Transcript*. This costs $480 a year but is available in many libraries.

Art Investment Guide, Pond House, Weybridge, Surrey, England. Quarterly. $30 a year. Editor, Richard Hislop.

A 20–28-page illustrated journal of informed comment on the art market; offshoot of *The Monthly Art Sales Index*. See Primary Reference Directories.

Art Letter, 150 E. 58 St., New York, NY 10022. Monthly. $28 a year; $50, two years; single copy, $3. Editor, Lee Rosenbaum.

Six-page newsletter subtitled "Art World Intelligence for Professionals."

Art News, 122 E. 42 St., New York, NY 10017. Monthly. Cir., 50,000. $18 a year. Editor, Milton Estorow.

Profiles, trends. Free-lance articles. For those dealing in paintings. For those interested in antiques, see *Antiques World*.

Canadi-Antiquer, Box 250, Chesley, Ontario N0G 1L0, Canada. Monthly tabloid. Cir., 12,000. $6 a year, Canada; $9 other. Editor, Jack Morrish.

Show sales and market news on increasingly active Canadian scene. Prolific, knowledgeable antiques free lance Bill Saks is a regular contributor. Classified section.

Chesapeake Antique Journal, P.O. Box 500, Warwick, MD 21912. Monthly tabloid. Cir., 10,000. $8.50 a year. Editor, Betty Speers.

Since combining with *National Antiques Courier,* the Maryland focus has expanded to national coverage ads. Uses free-lance contributions and runs ads from a column inch at $3.20 to full page for $18. Paper all black and white but will do color ads on request.

Clarion, 49 W. 53 St., New York, NY 10022. Quarterly. Museum of American Folk Art subscription membership, $20. Editor, Patricia Coblentz.

An example of nonprofit museum publication grown sleek and fat with ads and scholarly articles. See Chapter 8.

Collector, Drawer C, Kermit, TX 79745. Monthly tabloid. Cir., 43,267. $4, six months; $7.50 a year; $14, two years; single copy, 75¢.

Collectibles interests with lots of limited-edition and service-product ads and large classified section.

Collector Editions Quarterly, 170 Fifth Ave., New York, NY 10010. Five issues a year. Cir., 81,000. $8.50 for one year; $15, two years; single issue, $2.50.

Glossy magazine incorporating *Acquire.* Lot of ads for limited editions. This publisher also puts out a digest-sized bimonthly for miniature fans, *The Miniature Collector.*

Collector's Guide, City Magazines, Ltd., 1–3 Wine Office Court, Fleet St., London, EC4A 3A1, England. Monthly. Cir., 20,000. $25 a year. Editor, A. Brand.

This is the magazine that Mary Colby (Chapter 2) cites as the very best of the 19 publications she takes: "I sell a lot of fine old English furniture and this magazine is for dealers; gives prices and beautiful photos."

Collector's Journal, Box 601, Vinton, IA 52349. Weekly tabloid. $12.50 a year; $21, two years; $32, three years. Editor, Keith Knaack.

Weekly auction, antiques, and collectors' news for Midwest. Mostly local writing, except for syndicated Kovels' column.

Collectors News, 606 8th Ave., Grundy Center, IA 50638. Monthly tabloid. Cir., 30,000. $7.50 a year; $13.50, two years; single issue, 75¢. Editor, Mary Crocker.

Emphasizes collectibles interests; fat with ads. Lots and lots of classified throughout, with full-page ads going for $210, but $168 for cash. Uses short free-lance news pieces at 50¢-per-inch rates.

Connoisseur, National Magazine Co. Ltd., England. American edition, 250 W. 55 St., New York, NY 10019. Monthly. Cir., 17,500. $48 a year; $85, two years; single issue, $5. Editor, Joseph T. Butler.

One of the oldest magazines catering to fine collecting interests. International focus. Background articles, market news, ads.

Country Americana Magazine, P.O. Box 247, 13 Cornish St., Washington, NJ 07882. Bimonthly. $3.50 a year; 60¢, single issue. Editor, K. N. Cressman.

Pocket-sized national magazine; more nostalgia than collecting. One hundred percent consumer-oriented.

Early American Life, P.O. Box 1831, Harrisburg, PA 17105. Bimonthly. Cir., 260,000. $8 a year, with membership in Early American Society. Editor, Robert G. Miner.

Nationally focused toward those who buy reproductions and shop in country stores (where it's often sold), as well as collectors of originals. Traditional artisans often run small ads here.

Flea Market Quarterly, Box 243, Bend, OR 97701. Cir., 15,000. $6 a year; $2, single issue. Editor, Kenneth Asher.

Quarterly directory with some filler articles and ads for products directed to interests of flea market dealers.

Flea Market USA, Rt. 1, #470, Cantonment, FL 32533. $5 a year; $1.50, single copy.

Quarterly directory to 41 states. There are a number of other quarterly and annual flea market guides. Most weekly and monthly tabloids carry announcements as well.

Gray Letter, P.O. Drawer 2, Tuscaloosa, AL 35401. Weekly newsletter. $55 a year. Editor, Gray Boone.

Antique Monthly's editor-publisher launched this 4-page insider's report as extra service to at least some of the paper's readers. To date, close to a thousand have subscribed.

Hobbies, 10006 So. Michigan Ave., Chicago, IL 60605. Monthly. Cir., 46,000. $7 a year; $1, single issue. Editor, Ann Reeder.

Long-established national magazine with many repeat advertisers.

Helen Grey (Chapter 8) reports that lots of orders for her stationery designs come from her ads in this magazine.

International Art Market, pub. by *Art in America,* 150 E. 58 St., New York, NY 10022. Monthly. $40 a year; $70, two years. Editor, Howard L. Katzander.

Illustrated newsletter to which many high-income professionals seem to subscribe. Editor Katzander is an outspoken commentator.

Jersey Devil, New Egypt Auction and Farmers Market, Route 537, New Egypt, NJ 08533. Monthly tabloid. $6 a year, by mail (free on site). Editor, Fritz Davis.

Jersey-based and -focused news for and about flea marketers. Lots of ads.

Kovels on Antiques and Collectibles, Box 222000, N. Beachwood, OH 44122. Monthly. $20 a year; $35, two years. Editors, Ralph and Terry Kovel.

This newsletter publication marks yet another step up the ladder of super success for the indefatigable Kovels.

Magazine Antiques, Straight Enterprises, 551 Fifth Ave., New York, NY 10017. Monthly. Cir., 82,000. $24 a year; $42, two years; single issue, $3. Editor, Wendell Garrett.

This is one of the prestige magazines in the business. High ad rates call for high-quality merchandise. One dealer interviewed sold 4 chairs from an ad.

Maine Antiques Digest, Box 358, Waldoboro, ME 04572. Monthly tabloid. Cir., 13,000. $11.50 a year; $1, single issue. Editor, Samuel C. Pennington.

Maine and other New England antiques scene presented to a very devoted national audience. Advertising rates are bargain-priced from $2.50 for column inch to $150 for a full page, with the *Digest* developing and printing up advertisers' photos at cost. Free-lance articles used. (See Chapter 7.)

New York Antiques Almanac, Eye Publishing Co., Box 335, Lawrence, NY 11559. Monthly tabloid. Cir., 11,000. $6 a year; single issue, 75¢. Editor, Carol Nadel.

Regional news coverage. Editor seems to enjoy humor and runs a regular column by Joe Stamps. See Chapter 3.

New York–Pennsylvania Collector, 4 So. Main St., Pittsford, NY 14534. Cir., 10,000. $5 a year; single issue, 50¢. Editor, Nancy W. Bolger.

Focus on antiques, arts, and antiquarian books in New York–Pennsylvania area, though subscriptions go to 40 states. Nice graphics, articles. Lots of ads, ranging from $2.24 an inch to $130 for a full page, plus classifieds.

Ohio Antique Review, P.O. Box 538, Worthington, OH 43085. Monthly. $8 a year; single issue, 90¢. Editor, Pete Lauder.

Magazine subtitled *The Place for Americana.*

Relics, Western Publishing, Box 3338, Austin, TX 78746. Bimonthly. Cir., 5500. $2.50 a year; $4.50, two years; 35¢, single issue.

Spinoff from this publisher's Western magazines. Americana collectibles interests (not antiques). Free-lance articles at 2¢-per-word rate.

Spinning Wheel, American Antiques and Craft Society, Fame Ave., Hanover, PA 17331. Monthly. Cir., 35,000. $6 a year; single issue, $1. Editor, Albert Christian Revi.

National-interest magazine — antiques, collectibles. Display and classified ads. Free-lance material paid for by inch. See Chapter 7.

Tri-State Trader, P.O. Box 90, Knightstown, IN 46148. Weekly tabloid. Cir., 27,898. $8.25 a year; single issue, 40¢. Editor, Kevin Tanzillo.

Newspaper covering hobby, antique, auction, and collectors news for Ohio, Kentucky, Indiana, Michigan, Illinois, western Pennsylvania, West Virginia, Tennessee, Wisconsin, Missouri. Free-lance articles. Ads from classified to full page.

ARCHITECTURE, INTERIOR DESIGN, CRAFTS, CONSERVATION, AND RESTORATION PERIODICALS

Architectural Digest, 5900 Wilshire Blvd., Los Angeles, CA 90036. Nine issues a year. Cir., 330,000. $24.95 a year; single issue, $3. Editor, Paige Rense.

Many successful dealers cite this one as an excellent indicator of interior design trends all over the world. A full year's run, like many antiques magazines, is considered collectible in and of itself.

Crafts Horizon, 44 W. 53 St., New York, NY 10019. Bimonthly. Cir., 4000. $18 a year; includes membership in American Crafts Council. Editor, Rose Slivka.

The magazine for anyone who wants to keep abreast of who's who and what's what in the type of fine contemporary crafts that have been accepted by sophisticated collectors. International in scope. Museum, show, and gallery coverage, as well as in-depth write-ups on artists.

Gift and Decorative Accessories, 51 Madison Ave., New York, NY 10010. Monthly. $13 a year.

Trade magazine of the gift trade. Gift and accessory trends.

Guild of Book Workers Journal, 1059 Third Ave., New York, NY 10021. Three issues a year, $36, includes guild membership.

Guild news, articles on bookbinders and techniques.

Old-House Journal, 199 Berkeley Pl., Brooklyn, NY 11217. Monthly. $12 a year; $1.50, single copy. Editor, Clem Labine.

Illustrated newsletter-type publication about restoration and maintenance techniques for the old house, published and edited by Brooklyn brownstone dwellers. Newsletter itself has no advertising, but editors publish an insert of classified ads called "Old-House Emporium"; also an annual catalogue, which lists selected restorers and services free of charge.

Technology & Conservation of Art, Architecture and Antiquities, 1 Emerson Pl., Boston, MA 02114. Quarterly. $8 a year, $13 outside U.S. and Canada. Editor, Susan E. Schur.

Glossy magazine, international in focus, covering analysis, preservation, restoration, protection, documentation. Audience appeal is international, to professionals in the field. Lots of product information with reader service cards and calendar of professional meetings and seminars. Highly recommended by Ken Linsner, Chapter 6.

PRIMARY REFERENCE DIRECTORIES

AB Bookman's Yearbook, Antiquarian Bookman, Box AB, Clifton, NJ 02005.

Two-part directory to antiquarian trade by publisher of *AB Bookman's Weekly,* a trade magazine for anyone with antiquarian interests.

Antiques and Collectibles: A Bibliography of Works in English, 16th Century to 1976, Linda Campbell Franklin, The Scarecrow Press, Inc., Metuchen, NJ 08840, & London, 1978.

1091 pp, subject index of over 2800 subjects, divided into classifications, with bibliographic information for nearly 10,000 books and exhibition catalogues, and including library location guide.

Ayer Directory of Publications, 210 W. Washington Sq., Philadelphia, PA 19106

"*Ayer's*" is a vital reference for anyone who advertises. Directory gives area demography and explains basis for circulation figures: a particular mark indicates figures are taken at face value from publisher; publication's name in bold print means information is sworn to; outside audits are indicated by other symbols. Updated annually.

Books in Print, R. R. Bowker, 1180 Avenue of the Americas, New York, NY 10036. Annual.

About 450,000 books in print in the U.S.

Bowker Catalogue, 1180 Avenue of the Americas, New York, NY 10036.

The Bowker Company has extended its expertise about books on book publishing to many related areas, including antiques-collecting and antiquarian books. Their catalogue describing books mentioned here, plus lots of others, is free for the asking.

Contemporary Crafts Market Place, American Crafts Council, R. R. Bowker Co., 1180 Avenue of the Americas, New York, NY 10036.

Regularly updated directory of contemporary crafts galleries, studios, courses, books, more.

Dictionary of the Decorative Arts, John Fleming and Hugh Honour, Harper & Row, New York, NY 10036. 896 pages; more than 1000 black-and-white illustrations.

One of the most recently published references of this type. Older and often recommended: *The Oxford Companion to Art* and *The Oxford Companion to the Decorative Arts,* by Oxford University Press.

Encyclopedia of Associations, Gale Research Company, Book Tower, Detroit, MI 48226.

Mind-boggling array of all kinds of special-interest groups, both hobby and professionals. Some you may wish to join; newsletters of others offer well-targeted market for promotion and advertising. If you are planning to start your own organization, keep in mind the *Encyclopedia;* it is updated regularly and listings are free.

International Antiques Yearbook, Chestergate House, Vauxhall Bridge Rd., London SW IV IHF. Also in some libraries and U.S. bookshops. U.S. advertising, % Hearst Magazines, 224 W. 57 St., New York, NY 10019.

Directory of dealers, packers, shippers, auctioneers, salesrooms throughout the world. Also, associations and periodicals.

International Auction Records, Editions Publisol, 18 rue Danou, Paris 2, France. In United States, Box 239, 235 E. 8 St., New York, NY 10028.

Over 15,000 auction records in 5 separate sections: paintings, watercolors, drawings, prints, sculpture.

Lyle Official Reviews, Glenmayne, Galashiels, Selkirkshire, Scotland.
Illustrations, details, and values of thousands of items. Separate volumes on art, antiques, and arms and armor.

Monthly Art Sales Index, Pond House, Weybridge, Surrey, England.
Computerized record of auction sales of paintings. A bound annual, *Annual Art Sales Index,* is also published here; as is a quarterly magazine, *Art Investment Guide.* See Chapter 7, pages 141–142, for profile of publisher.

Subject Guide to Books in Print, R. R. Bowker, 1180 Avenue of the Americas, New York, NY 10036. Annual.
Looking for a book on a particular subject? Planning to write a book? This is the place to check what's out in the U.S.

Ulrich's International Periodicals Directory, R. R. Bowker, 1180 Avenue of the Americas, New York, NY 10036.
International index to magazines on every conceivable subject, with names of editors and circulation figures.

World Market Auction Records, Sotheby Parke Bernet, Inc., 980 Madison Ave., New York, NY 10021.
Individual sale records with prices. Other major auction houses also publish similar records.

Writer's Market, Writer's Digest, 9933 Alliance Road, Cincinnati, OH 45242.
Publishing opportunities — book and magazine — with information geared to novice writers. Updated annually.

BACKGROUND, BUSINESS, AND MISCELLANEOUS BOOKS AND BOOKLETS

Since Part I of this book spotlights the people behind the objects, Part II concentrates on publications that will help them function more successfully, rather than on specific antiques books. Details on these can be found in the publications listed under the Art-Antiques-Collectibles Press and Primary Reference Directories.

American Society of Appraisers. P.O. Box 17265, Washington, DC 20041. See Chapter 13 for this organization's publications.

Antiques and Restoration. Research Park, Cornell University, Ithaca, NY 14853.
 Packet of 9 bulletins on various restoration topics, published by university's school of human ecology, and available for $3.00.

The Art Game. Robert Wraight. New York: Simon and Schuster, 1965.
 Interesting overview of the art market by former London art critic and correspondent.

Art on the Market. Maurice Rheims. London: George Weidenfeld and Nicolson Ltd., 1969 (translation).
 Well-known Parisian auctioneer and valuer's assessment of 35 centuries of art collecting and collectors. Discussion of different collectors and their predilections makes entertaining and enlightening reading.

Auction. James Bough. Indianapolis, IN: Bobbs-Merrill Co., Inc., 1973.
 Fascinating chronicle of the history of auctions and the great auction houses — for buyer and auctioneer alike.

Business Planning Guide. David H. Bangs and William R. Osgood. The Federal Reserve Bank of Boston, 30 Pearl St., Boston, MA 02106. $1.00.

Ninety-six-page workbook to help those people who are preparing a detailed business plan.

Cousin Pons, Part 2 of *Poor Relations.* Honoré de Balzac. Great Britain: Penguin Books, 1978.
Novelist Balzac's masterly study of a passionate collector and the nineteenth-century Paris antiques scene. Great insight into the collector's psyche, and a "good read," as well.

Economics of Taste, Parts I, II, III. Gerald Reitlinger. London: Barrie & Jenkins Ltd., 1960 through 1970.
Though the price information in these exhaustive studies of art and antiques is out of date, the introductory writing remains valuable to an understanding of fluctuations in, and determination of, prices.

The Elegant Auctioneers. Wesley Towner. New York: Hill and Wang, 1970.
Occasionally reads like a company-ordered biography of Sotheby Parke Bernet, but nevertheless a well-drawn picture of big-time auctioneering and its evolution.

How Mail Order Fortunes Are Made. Alfred Stern. New York: Arco Press, 1977.
If you can get past the "hype" you'll find some useful tips.

How to Get Big Results from a Small Advertising Budget. Cynthia S. Smith. New York: Hawthorn Books, 1973.
Not addressed to the antiques advertiser, as few general business books are, but there's a lot of adaptable information in this handy paperback.

How to Organize a Small Business. Clifford M. Baumbach, Kenneth Lawyer, and Pearce C. Kelley. Englewood Cliffs, NJ: Prentice-Hall, Inc., 1973.
More a textbook than a layman's manual, but filled with solid, general business information.

How to Run a Small Business. J. K. Lasser. New York: McGraw-Hill Book Co., Inc., 1963.

There have been many laymen's guides to business since this one appeared, but it remains an excellent guide, with sections entitled Going into Business, Managing and Operating Your Business, Managing of Special Business.

How to Save Money on Your Telephone Bills. Arthur S. Curtis. 816 National Press Building, Washington, DC 20045. $1.50.

Sixty-four–page paperback by president of Telephone Users Association, aimed primarily at small business person.

Instructions for Mailers. U.S. Postal Service Publication, Superintendent of Documents, U.S. Government Printing Office, Washington, DC 20402.

Regularly updated guide to postal rules and regulations, for volume mailers, available on a subscription basis for $5.00 a year.

The Making of the Annotated Directory of Self-Published Textile Books. Elyse Sommer. Box E, Woodmere, NY, 1978.

Twenty-five cents in stamps or coin and a stamped, addressed envelope brings 2-page history of how one small publication was published and distributed by author: pricing, production, copyright, ISBN, etc.

Packing for Mailing. U.S. Government Printing Office, Washington, DC 20402 or local post office.

Free illustrated booklet . . . and very good, indeed!

"Parson's Pleasure," from *Kiss, Kiss*. Roald Dahl. New York: Alfred Knopf, 1953 (also as a paperback, Dell Publishing Co.).

Short-story writer Dahl's sparkling humor will make even those who grumble most about upgrading the antique dealer's image chuckle at this deft portrait of a wily London dealer.

Preservation and Tax Reform Act of 1976. Archeology and Historic Preservation Office, Department of the Interior, Washington, DC 20240.

Free information about taxes, depreciation, etc., for anyone in a building that may fall within preservation certification.

Small Business Administration, 1441 L St., N.W., Washington, DC 20416
List of helpful publications available either by mail or from your local SBA office is extensive. *Starting and Managing a Small Business, Selecting the Legal Structure for Your Firm,* and *Staffing Your Store* are just some.

Small Business Reporter, Bank of America, Dept. 3120, Box 3700, San Francisco, CA 94137.
A request for free catalogue will bring another list of dozens of inexpensive booklets helpful for the small business.

Small-Time Operator: How to Start Your Own Small Business, Keep Your Books, Pay Your Taxes and Stay Out of Trouble, a Guide and Workbook. Bernard Kamaroff. Box 322, Laytonville, CA 95454, 1976.
People who hate business books will find this workbook approach by a C.P.A. more palatable than most. A sample business is an antiques shop. Soft-cover edition available.

Tax Guide for Small Business, Publication 334, Internal Revenue Service, U.S. Government Printing Office, Washington, DC 20402.
Issued annually to help small business person.

Up Your Own Organization. Donald M. Dibble. Santa Clara, CA: The Entrepreneur Press, 1974. Distributed by Hawthorn Books, Inc., 260 Madison Ave., New York, NY 10016.
Large-size, easy-to-follow paperback on business procedures.

You Inc.: A Detailed Escape Route to Being Your Own Boss. Peter Weaver. New York: Doubleday and Co., 1975.
More inspirational than how-to-do-it, this is nevertheless a good book for those seeking a different lifestyle or second career in the antiques business.

CHAPTER 10

❖ ❖ ❖

Advertising
and Promotion
Guidelines

HOW TO USE THE PRESS RELEASE TO OBTAIN
FREE COVERAGE

Opening a shop, launching a catalogue, or announcing a show —
all this is news, even though the purpose of the story is to benefit
your organization. As long as you present your message with the
editor's need for news in mind, write in a straightforward manner
without a lot of self-serving adjectives, it will be printed as news.
Don't ignore small media, including organizations' newsletters.

How to Prepare a News Release

1. Type and double space, using 8½-by-11-inch paper.
2. Put "For Immediate Release" or the date on which you want the
story to break in the upper left-hand corner; the word "Contact,"
followed by your name, address, and phone number in the right.
3. Answer the following questions immediately: Who, what,
where, when, and why. Get it all into one paragraph. Follow this
with additional information, but confine yourself to two pages. The

more it reads like a story and can be used exactly as is, the better your chances of having it all used.

4. Address your release to the editor. Be sure you spell the name right.

5. If the story calls for it, include a photograph. Do not write on the photograph. Type up an identifying caption on the bottom half of a sheet of paper, glue the blank portion, with rubber cement, to the back of the photo, and fold up over photo.

HOW TO GET THE MOST FROM ADVERTISING DOLLARS

1. As a general rule, the biggest ad you can afford is the best.

2. Repeat, repeat, repeat. One-time ads seldom get results. Repetition also applies to the typeface you use and the place where you put your name and address. These become your "signature."

3. People like to see what you have to offer. Photographs are particularly important if advertised merchandise is not clearly identifiable through the copy, has a high price tag, and if the ad is expensive.

4. Gear ad contents to the medium and the copy to the reader's needs. In short, advertise merchandise the reader of a particular publication would be likely to use and give the reader a reason for wanting it.

5. Research the media. Read sample copies, check circulation figures with publisher and through *Ulrich's* and *Ayer's* (see Primary Reference Directories). Remember to look up collectors'-group publications for inexpensive and very direct targeting (see *Encyclopedia of Associations*).

6. Check your layout for "gaze motion," an advertising term describing the way the ad is designed to direct the reader's eye to the key elements. The headline should be the starting and focal element.

7. Classified ads are most effective in periodicals where such sections are regular, well-read features. Since rates are per word, check and recheck copy for word conservation. Use dashes and ellipses to take place of costly words, and use white space, which creates illusion of size. Familiarize yourself with proven phrases such as "free,"

"how to," "new," "money-back." Make the first few words grab the reader for the rest of the ad and end with words that will lead to specific action. If a classified ad is run regularly, change around at least the first few words; don't repeat the same wording over and over.

8. If you run an ad in more than one place, be sure to key it so that you can keep tabs on which medium works best. This means adding a department number or letter to your address.

CHAPTER 11

❖ ❖ ❖

Photography
Know-How

The ability to take clear, well-focused pictures is useful in almost any type of antiques-collectibles endeavor. Reasonably priced, easy-to-use basic equipment is within everyone's means.

Basic Equipment

1. A single lens reflex 35 mm. camera that takes interchangeable lenses.
2. Flash attachments for "on location" pictures.
3. Tripod, if you move around a lot — a regular and a smaller portable model.
4. Four floodlights and two stands to hold two lights each.
5. One roll of white and one roll of black photography background paper; a roll of gray and some other colors if you do many color slides.

Developing and Printing Pictures

1. Establish contact with a camera shop that has on-site custom printing service.

2. Always have a proof sheet made from which you can select final prints and which can be used as a record for additional prints to be made up at a future date.

3. For color pictures, slides, kept in plastic pockets, are preferable (especially for any type of reproduction) to prints.

Taking Pictures

1. Avoid distracting backgrounds.

2. Take three shots at three different f-stop exposures. For example, if you are focused on 4.5, take another shot at 4.0 and one at 5.0.

3. Use Panatomic-X film for black-and-white prints; Ektachrome for color slides.

CHAPTER 12

❖ ❖ ❖

Legal Matters

Agreements covering consignments and merchandise rentals, option buying, and finder fee arrangements should always be put in writing. They can be quite simple, in the form of a letter or memorandum, or can be set up in more formal style. The forms that follow contain some of the points to be included. Depending on the arrangements you will be making, you can add or delete certain stipulations.

Consignment Agreement

Made between _____

and _____

on _____ *19* _____.

_____ *and* _____

hereinafter known as Consignor and Consignee respectively agree that:

1. Consignor shall offer for sale the following merchandise belonging to Consignee:

2. The Consignor's commission for a sale will be _____ percent of the retail price.

3. Retail price shall be no less than _____.

4. Merchandise shall be left for a minimum of _____ and a maximum of _____.

5. Consignor will pay Consignee _____ after date of sale.

6. If merchandise remains unsold after above-stated minimum period and Consignee requests its return, Consignor shall have the option to buy at _____.

7. Ownership of merchandise resides with the Consignee and cannot be transferred to the creditors of the Consignor.

_____   _____
Signature   *Signature*

Rental Agreement

Renting antiques for use by magazine stylists, television set designers, or advertising agencies is a welcome and lucrative opportunity, available primarily in large cities. Ten percent of the purchase price is a commonly used fee basis. Even if you lend merchandise on a quid pro quo publicity trade-off basis, it's best to protect yourself with some written form regarding responsibility and safe return.

On _____ *19*_____

_____

agrees to allow _____
to use the following merchandise:

for a minimum number of _____ *days and a maximum of*
_____ *days, at a fee of* _____ *per day* (per diem can be changed to flat fee) *payable on* _____. *The replacement value of the merchandise is* _____. *In the event of loss, theft, or damage, rentee will pay the renter full replacement value.*

_____   _____
Signature   *Signature*

Option Buying Agreement

Option agreement made between _____

and _____

on _____ *19* _____.

_____ *and* _____

hereinafter known as Buyer and Seller, agree that:
1. *In consideration of the sum of* _____, *payable upon signing of this agreement, Buyer shall have the right to purchase from Seller the following merchandise:*

for the sum of _____.
2. *If Buyer does not exercise option to buy by* _____ *19____, this agreement will no longer be effective.*

(Option payment can be applicable to purchase price, or an override payment.)

_____   _____
Signature   *Signature*

Finder's Fee Confirmation

Dear _____ :
        (name of contact at auction house)
        This is to confirm our conversation of _____
19_____, *in which you agreed to take the following*
property:

owned by _____
as a consignment for auction. A commission of _____
percent of the total profit realized will be paid to me
upon conclusion of the sale.

        I am sending a copy of this agreement along with this
letter for your cosignature. A copy is also going to _____
_____ .

_____
Dealer's signature

_____
Auction house countersignature.

CHAPTER 13

❖ ❖ ❖

People and Places
for Guidance
and Education

EDUCATIONAL OPPORTUNITIES

At present, only schools with art history and graduate conservation studies (see Chapter 6), leading to curatorial careers, offer formal degrees. Nevertheless, opportunities abound for those who want to be better qualified as antiques professionals. College extension and adult education courses, seminars and conferences, varying in cost as well as quality, proliferate. The following are mere samplings of trends.

1. Appraisal studies combined as a specialty discipline within an art history degree program, like the one at Hofstra University, Hempstead, New York.

2. Certificate appraisal programs. Examples are the ones at the C. W. Post branch of Long Island University, in Greenvale, and Hofstra in Hempstead, both in New York.

3. Courses that use major auction houses as classrooms. There are Sotheby Parke Bernet's and Christie Manson and Wood's London-

based fine arts courses, and less costly, part-time opportunities at Hunter College's Lifelong Learning Center in New York City. The latter institution has also sponsored two-day intensive business seminars for antiques professionals, held at hotels throughout the country.

4. Auctioneering courses specifically slanted to the art and antiques professional, like the summer courses at the University of Massachusetts in South Deerfield, Massachusetts, given in conjunction with the International Auction School of Louisville, Kentucky. Near the university, Historic Deerfield, which operates twenty restored properties, offers summer fellowships for college students, to encourage museum careers.

Since all adult education programs and seminars fluctuate with student needs and demand, it's a good idea to check announcements each season. The announcements are usually carried in major art-antiques-collectibles publications. The organizations described in the next section will lead to other opportunities.

ORGANIZATIONS

The following listing includes organizations open to all types of memberships and eager to provide educational guidance as well as some that are fairly closed and selective groups, somewhat like the medieval crafts guilds, which were formed primarily for the benefit of an exclusive membership.

American Antiquarian Society, 185 Salisbury St., Worcester, MA 01609.

Founded in 1822, with 320 members and a staff of 30, the society boasts a research library of almost five million books, broadsides, manuscripts, prints, maps, and newspapers. Reading rooms are open to the public without charge. Newsletter by subscription, $20 a year.

American Association of Museums, 1055 Thomas Jefferson St., N.W., Washington, DC 20007. Richard McLanathan, Director.

National organization with regional groups. Six thousand members from diverse museum energies. A clearinghouse of information that sponsors seminars and programs for museum personnel, conducts tours, maintains a placement service for museum professionals. Monthly newsletter and bimonthly publication, *Museum News,* by subscription.

American Crafts Council, 29 W. 53 St., New York, NY 10022.

Research and reference department, open to the public, for help in locating courses in all types of crafts and in studying professional artist slide files. Numerous publications and slide kits available. Membership fee of $18 brings bimonthly *Crafts Horizons* magazine.

American Institute for Conservation of Historic and Artistic Works, 1522 K Street, N.W., Suite 804, Washington, DC 20005.

Associate memberships open to anyone interested in field of conservation brings monthly newsletter and semiannual journal for $20. Journal alone, $15. Fellowship members must have five years of experience as practicing professionals.

American Society of Appraisers, P.O. Box 17265, Washington, DC 20041.

Membership subject to passing various tests. Educational materials available to all. See Chapter 4 on appraising.

Antiquarian Booksellers Association of America, 630 Fifth Ave., Shop 2, Concourse, New York, NY 10020.

Professional organization. Membership list available to anyone interested in contacting members.

Appraisers Association of America, 541 Lexington Ave., New York, NY 10022.

Membership subject to experience and recommendation. See Chapter 4 on appraising.

Art and Antique Dealers League of America, 5 E. 66 St., New York, NY 10021.

One hundred and twenty members, all retail dealers. Membership list available.

Art Dealers Association of America, 575 Madison Ave., New York, NY 10022.
Members are all art dealers.

British Antique Dealers Association, Ltd., 20 Rutland Gate, London SW7 1 BD, England.
Names and addresses of members available.

Canadian Antique Dealers' Association, Box 517, Station K, Toronto 12, Ontario, Canada.
See *International Antiques Yearbook,* under Primary Reference Directories, for dealers' associations in other countries.

Decorative Arts Trust, New Hope, PA 18938.
Nationwide membership organization that serves as clearinghouse for speakers, donations, restoration, and other information. Membership, $15 a year.

Guild of Bookworkers, 1059 Third Ave., New York, NY 10021.
Membership open to hobbyists and professionals. Guild maintains list of professional bookbinders and publishes a leaflet (price, $1) listing study opportunities. Membership fee of $36 includes journal, issued three times a year.

Investment Research Center, 380 Avenue Louise, 1050 Brussels, Belgium. Prof. J. A. Horn, Director.
Schedules conferences on art investment.

National Antique and Art Dealers Association of America, 59 E. 57 St., New York, NY 10022.
Very small (46 members) exclusive dealers' group.

National Association of Dealers in Antiques, Inc., 7080 Old River Rd., RR 6, Rockford, IL 61103.

Eight hundred carefully screened members who are shop, mail order, and show dealers. National convention and monthly bulletin, which several members who were interviewed find very helpful. Members receive cards and certificate with organization emblem and slogan: "Antiquity with Integrity."

National Auctioneers Association, 135 Lakewood Dr., Lincoln, NB 68510

Member auctioneers receive magazine published eleven times a year, membership list, and chance to partake in conventions and meetings. Fee, $20.

National Trust for Historic Preservation, 740 Jackson Place, N.W., Washington, DC 20006.

A nonprofit national organization for preserving history, neighborhoods, buildings, with memberships of all types and many interesting publications and educational opportunities. Literature detailing all activities is free.

Victorian Society in America, E. Washington Sq., Philadelphia, PA 19106.

Four thousand members with shared interest in nineteenth century. They run lectures, slide programs, organize exhibits, discussions, and tours. In addition to a monthly bulletin, $15 membership brings beautiful quarterly magazine, *Nineteenth Century*.

❖ ❖ ❖

Glossary of Antiques Trade Jargon

Absentee bid: Buyer unable to attend sale leaves bid, with or without deposit. Theoretically, auction employee or auctioneer bids for the absentee bidder, though he often uses the bid to run price up to and past it.

Adaptation: New use for functionally outmoded objects; e.g., a lamp made from a crock.

Advance: Upward price steps at an auction sale, anywhere from fifty cents to $500 at a step. Also, money advanced by a dealer to a picker or scout, and, at times, by an auctioneer to a dealer in need of quick cash.

Advanced collector: One who is knowledgeable about his collecting field.

After: Euphemism for a copy; e.g., "after Chippendale" is a piece made in that manner but not by the master. "Manner of" means same thing.

Age: Important value criterion, though meaningless if date is not associated with quality and desirability, or if condition is poor or restoration excessive.

Agent: Free-lance or salaried buyer for private party, dealer, or auctioneer. When agent travels the garage sale and flea market circuit, he is a *Picker;* when dealer bids for private customer at auction, he is usually called an agent.

All or choice: An auction offering at which pieces in numbered lot can be bought in entirety — all — or by the piece — choice.

Alteration: See *Adaptation.*

Antiquarian: Any student of antiquities; e.g., the antiquarian bookman.

Antique: From the Latin for "very old." By customs definition, generally anything 100 years old. In comparison with other types of commodities, a nonreproducible, nonessential item, with value determined by taste and demand.

Antiquer: Colloquial for collector. Though dictionary makes no reference to a verb form, "let's go antiquing" has enjoyed common usage.

Antiquary: Expert on, or collector of, antiquities or ancient objects. Latin in origin; concerned with relics.

Antiquity: Older than antique; predating Middle Ages.

Appraiser: One who evaluates the worth of property to meet a specific need; e.g., to arrive at *fair market value.*

Archival value: Those qualities which make an object worth preserving.

Ascribed to: Less than positive identification of the maker of an object.

As is: Describing condition of a sale. What you see — and what you fail to see — is what you get!

Attic dealer: One who sells from home without shop sign.

Attributed to: See *Ascribed to.*

Attribution: Proof about the maker and general history of a piece.

Auctioneer: Person who conducts auction sale.

Auction bookkeeper: Person who keeps record of each item sold during auction.

Authentic: Exactly as represented; e.g., a genuine Chippendale chair, without any hidden repairs.

Bid: Price offered. Can apply to any kind of a sale, from tag sale to auction.

Bid pulling: Method of delaying final *Knockdown* or sale at an auction; opposite of *Quick knock.*

Black light: Fluorescent light that scans out repairs.

Blue-chip antiques: Objects, unaffected by taste trends, of sufficiently high basic and increasing value to be safely equated with other types of investments.

Bought-in: Consigned merchandise at an auction that did not reach agreed-upon *Reserve* and was bought back in, left as unsold in the marked catalogue issued by auctioneer.

Bric-a-brac: Small items of decorative and sentimental value.

Broker: One who follows around foreign buyer, packs, ships, insures purchases.

Buy-back: Dealer's offer to buy back merchandise sold to private customer, usually at 10 percent increase of price; a good-will gesture.

Buy cheap, sell dear: Old-time motto for successful trading.

By appointment or by chance: Sign frequently seen in shop windows or on business cards.

Caveat emptor: Latin for "Let the buyer beware." The warning means the seller does not guarantee the condition of merchandise.

Celebrity auction: Sale of possessions of well-known personality, designed to draw large crowds and high prices; e.g., "eyelashes and jewelry from estate of the late Joan Crawford," or "g-strings from personal wardrobe of the late Gypsy Rose Lee."

Chatchkas: Nationally recognized New Yorkese, originally Yiddish, for the more elegant term, *Bric-a-brac.*

Choice: The very best of its kind. See also *All or choice.*

Circa: Latin preposition, now used as English, meaning "about." So, about 1910 becomes circa 1910 or c. 1910. People in the trade use the word as a noun and talk of particular circas as being especially desirable; e.g., the circa spanning the years 1900 to 1910.

Circle of: Used in describing paintings identified with a master painter but probably painted by apprentices or students. "School of," "factory of," and "studio of" are similar expressions for secondary attribution.

Cluster shops: Retail antiques establishments grouped or clustered in one street, building, or neighborhood.

Codes: Dealer's method of tagging merchandise with letters or numbers instead of prices. No longer used by most modern dealers.

Collectible: Catchall for anything striking a collector's fancy, usually under 50 years old.

Collectibility: Defines potential of an object to gain popularity and value. Objects easily identified, not easy to reproduce, or available in sufficiently large but not inexhaustible quantities most readily meet collectibility criteria; e.g., *Limited editions.*

Collector-dealer: Someone who collects for personal use and pleasure but also sells, either to support collecting habit or as part-time vocation.

Combination: See *Ring.*

Commemorative: Anything made specifically to serve as reminder of a special event; e.g., Centennial items.

Commingling: Mixing functions. An appraiser able to evaluate paintings and furniture may be considered versatile or diversified; an appraiser who mixes valuation with buying and selling is commingling, and invites criticism on ethical grounds.

Condition: Functional and physical state of an object, and the extent to which this is original or repaired.

Connoisseur: One with critical expertise of things identified with fine quality.

Conservation: Science of caring for objects and thus preventing their decay and destruction.

Conservator: One trained in conservation and restoration techniques; functions include consultation about use of materials (such as paints and lacquers) for endurance, and recommendations as to care and treatment for disrepair.

Consignment: That which is sold on a commission basis, with the seller the middleman rather than the owner of the merchandise.

Container loads: Merchandise imported from abroad, bought in lots large enough to fill a shipping container.

Corporate collectible: Things from a firm's past with interest to social historians and collectors; old catalogues, containers, products, etc.

Corporate collector: One who collects for public or business spaces rather than private use.

Courier: One who drives foreign buyer around, usually employed by a *Broker.*

Dealer deals: Typified by co-investment in costly pieces, with dealers sharing sales responsibility and profit.

Dealer discount: Ranges from absorbing shipping costs to taking 30 percent off retail price; 15 percent the average.

Dealer-to-dealer buying: Large part of the trade; often done during shows and during closed-for-retail season.

Downgrading: A dealer's disparaging the value of an item, to drive down the price. Also known as *Hard selling.*

Dutch auction: Starts with top asking bid and works backward. First spoken bid takes merchandise.

Ephemera: Items created for short-term use; e.g., paper fans.

Facsimile: Reproduction of print, book, manuscript.

Fair market value: Price at which property will change hands between a willing buyer and a willing seller.

Firm price: Opposite of soft price. Dealers show no signs of lowering prices, and buyers are willing to pay whatever is asked.

Flea market: Indoor or outdoor market at which everything from fleas to antiques is sold; originated with famous Paris flea market.

Float buying: Buying where things are not highly valued, and selling them where they are.

Floor man: Person who helps to spot bids and handle merchandise at auction. In city auction houses, spotting and handling are two separate functions; in country auction houses, they are an all-in-one function. The term *Runner* is also common.

Generic collections: Broad-based categories that lend themselves to horizontal growth and diversification; for example, the textile collector can collect all types of textile objects, tools and equipment, and reading materials, or he can specialize in particular periods or objects. Professional specialist with generic specialty will have broader scope than one who starts and remains narrow.

Hard selling: See *Downgrading.*

Haulers: See *Pickers.*

Heirlooms: Younger than antiques, older than collectibles, usually 50 to 100 years old. Value is often determined by sentiment.

House Bid: See *Absentee bid.*

House pickers: See *Pickers.*

Inventory layaway: Dealers' practice of taking merchandise out of stock for purposes of an updated look and to await more favorable market.

Inventory turn: Number of times a dealer's stock of merchandise is sold in a given period of time.

Knockdown: Sold, as at auction.

Knockers: See *Pickers*

Knockoff: A modern copy.

Licensed appraiser: A false term since there is no licensing in the appraising profession.

Licensed auctioneer: Licenses meet local government specifications, not something earned, as a college degree.

Limited edition: An item whose production was limited to a given number, which can range from two to 20,000. Presumably, when a company completes a run of limited edition plates, the mold is destroyed.

Liquidation sale: Also known as priced liquidation and estate sales. All merchandise is marked with prices, as opposed to merchandise in an auction sale. It can be sold on premises of owner or seller or in rented space.

Liquidation value: Price an immediate sale would bring.

Lot: Merchandise units consisting of one or more items but grouped in one lot.

Mail auction: Sale held without salesroom or meeting of auctioneer and buyers. Items are described in catalogue, with estimated prices, and bids are returned by mail or phone.

Mall show: An antiques sale held in a shopping center, with dealers brought in by mall management as way of increasing traffic to mall and its regular stores.

Marks: Inscriptions, hallmarks, signatures, which clearly identify objects. Marked or signed pieces tend to be more valuable than others, provided marks are not faked.

Markup: Difference between the dealer's cost and retail price, anywhere from 10 percent for quick turnover to 100 percent, with 30 to 50 percent most common.

Markup determinants: Cost of acquisition, cost of selling, cost of replacement, rarity of item.

Married piece: An item that has had part of another added to it in the process of repair or restoration; e.g., a chair with legs "married from" another.

New collectible: Category created or promoted by an astute collector, dealer, or collector-dealer.

Nostalgia: Theme of collections, shows, or dealerships based on sentimental response to objects of the not-so-distant past.

Option buying: Ensuring right to buy something in future at present price by giving owner an option payment.

Pickers: Suppliers for dealers and auctioneers who pick up bargains wherever possible, either free-lance or to fill specific requests. Also known as *Knockers,* since they often knock on doors to ask if owner has anything to dispose of; or *Runners,* since they run all over the place; or *Haulers* if they haul stuff in trucks and pickups, often to great distances; or *House pickers* or *Scouts* when they buy with the dealer's money.

Pool: See *Ring.*

Price Codes: See *Codes.*

Price Guides: Printed estimates of current market values based on prices fetched for similar items. Because of variables of geography, condition, and, at times, biased view of the price gatherers, guides should not be regarded as absolutes.

Primitive: Simple, unsophisticated object, as distinct from work of trained artisans and artists.

Promoter: Organizer of antiques shows and flea markets.

Provenance: Source of origin, ownership, etc., based on available historic information.

Put and sell: Dealer's rule for buying, meaning that buyer must name selling price instead of dealer making an offer.

Quick knock: Rapping of gavel or hammer without the pause that would allow a final auction bid. Sellers or consigners like a slow knock; buyers prefer the quick knock.

Rentals: Objects lent to organizations, nonantiques stores, television studios, and magazine stylists for a fee, usually 10 percent of retail price.

Replacement value: Estimated cost of replacing something lost through fire or theft.

Reserve: Price agreed upon between auctioneer and consigner as the lowest bid accepted. If reserve is not reached, consigner can buy back merchandise.

Restoration: Anything from minor repair to major replacement or complete rebuilding, as in a restored village.

Restorer: One with restoration skills, ranging from repair and refinishing to conservator's technological know-how.

Right: "Is it right?" is an oft-heard question in regard to authenticity, amount and type of restoration.

Ring: Group of dealers who bid as one, then hold own sale. New England rings are known as *Pools.*

Room craft: Bidding shrewdness.

Runner: Traveling dealer or *Picker.* At country auctions, the runner is the *Floor man,* doing a little of everything.

Salting sales: Term for adding merchandise from sources other than property featured for a sale.

Scouts: See *Pickers.*

Selected additions: See *Salting sales.*

Shill: One who mingles with auctiongoers, before or during sale, to create high-price aura and drive up bidding.

Shipping goods: Imported merchandise ordered without personal selection. Dealers define succinctly: junk.

Show dealer: One without a shop, selling through shows.

Soft: Used to describe buyer resistance to asking prices, as in, "Prices are currently soft or sluggish."

Style: Form or look that identifies objects made during a particular period; e.g., art nouveau style of late nineteenth and early twentieth century. Style can be manifest in furnishings, architecture, and decorative accessories.

Swap meet: Term for flea markets in West.

Tag sales: All or part of the contents of private home tagged with selling prices; also known as garage and yard sales, according to setting.

Troy weight: System of weights for measuring precious metals.

Unreserved sale or *Unrestricted sale:* Everything goes, no matter how low the bid.

Utilitarian antiques and collectibles: Those which can either function as originally intended (e.g., furniture) or which can serve new uses.

❖ ❖ ❖

Index